During the early years of this century John Reed was the most highly-paid, ace reporter in the United States. He was a reporter during the First World War, and was in Petrograd in 1917, one of the few western witnesses to the Bolshevik Revolution. He was profoundly influenced by communist ideas and was a central figure in the foundation of the US communist party. He returned to Russia after the war but died in Moscow in 1920. He is buried in Red Square.

Ten Days That Shook the World
Insurgent Mexico

THE WAR IN EASTERN EUROPE

TRAVELS THROUGH THE BALKANS IN 1915

John Reed

Illustrations by Boardman Robinson

PHŒNIX

A PHOENIX PAPERBACK

First published by Scribners in 1916
This paperback edition first published in 1994 by Phoenix,
an imprint of Orion Books Ltd,
Orion House, 5 Upper St Martin's Lane,
London WC2H 9EA

© 1994 Orion Books Ltd

Reissued 1999

A CIP catalogue record for this book is available from
the British Library

ISBN: 0 75380 926 5

Set by Selwood Systems, Midsomer Norton
Printed and bound in Great Britain by
Butler & Tanner Ltd, Frome and London

CONTENTS

ILLUSTRATIONS

PUBLISHER'S NOTE

The Eastern phases of the war are by far the most confusing and uncertain – a book explaining the political or military situations in Russia, the Balkans, and Turkey, however sound at the time of acceptance for publication, would probably be utterly misleading when it came from the press. But while physical circumstances change, human nature never does; and it was chiefly with humanity that John Reed and Boardman Robinson were concerned when they travelled through these countries for the Metropolitan Magazine. Just as the novelist or the biographer presents the personality of a character so do they present the personality of a nation.

'As I look back on it all,' says Mr Reed, 'it seems to me that the most important thing to know about the war is how the different peoples live; their environment, tradition, and the revealing things they do and say. In time of peace, many human qualities are covered up which come to the surface in a sharp crisis; but on the other hand, much of personal and racial quality is submerged in time of great public stress. And in this book Robinson and I have simply tried to give our impressions of human beings as we found them in the countries of Eastern Europe, from April to October, 1915.'

So it is that though physical circumstances have in a number of instances changed in the fluctuations of political and military strife since this journey, the value of this account has not changed, but is now indeed enhanced by the increased importance of understanding what all these nations are and why and how they are fighting.

The book opens with a trip into Serbia, 'then devastated,' to quote the author, 'by typhus and slowly recovering from the frightful consequences of the last Austrian invasion.' This was just about the time of the great Russian Retreat. After that had begun, Mr Reed obtained, from the American Minister at Bucharest, a list of American citizens to look up and, with this as an excuse, he and Mr Robinson crossed the river Pruth at night in a small boat and landed at the Russian front. 'It was unprecedented. The orders were very strict that no correspondents should be allowed in these regions, but the orders specified correspondents coming from the north. We came from the south, and so, not knowing what to do with us, they sent us north. We travelled behind the Russian front through Bucovina, Galicia, and Poland.'

Naturally there were difficulties with the authorities and as a result of these after being arrested and released, Mr Reed and Mr Robinson journeyed to Petrograd; and the description of this journey across a landscape vast and grand in company with soldiers and officers will leave a permanent impression on the reader's mind – whenever he thinks of Russia he will be likely to envisage it accordingly.

'Once more in Bucharest,' says Mr Reed, 'I determined to see Constantinople, which seemed calmer and safer than ever. Robinson could not go because he had a British passport. Enver Pasha first promised me that I should go to the Gallipoli front; but after two weeks' waiting he said that no more Americans would be allowed with the army, because one correspondent had gone back to Paris and there published a description of the Turkish forts. About this same time I was unofficially notified that I had better leave Turkey, because the police had seen me talking with too many Armenians.'

Returning again to Bucharest, Mr Reed met Mr Robinson and then together they travelled through Bulgaria, then on the brink of war, and once more through Serbia, and after a few days' stay in Salonika they sailed for home.

The military operations they saw, except in the case of the Russian retreat, were not on the grand scale, 'and for that very reason, perhaps,' says Mr Reed, 'we were better able to observe the more normal life of the Eastern nations, under the steady strain of long-drawn-out warfare. In the excitement of sudden invasion, desperate resistance, capture and destruction of cities, men seem to lose their distinctive personal or racial flavour, and become alike in the mad democracy of battle. As we saw them, they had settled down to war as a business, had begun to adjust themselves to this new way of life and to talk and think of other things.'

Portions of the war of Eastern Europe, as originally published in book form related to personal adventures, such as the arrest of Mr Reed and Mr Robinson in Poland, their experiences with the Cossacks, and their entanglement in diplomatic red tape at Petrograd. These and certain chapters of a general nature, though in themselves highly interesting, have been omitted for the sake of compression and in view of the single purpose of the series – to enable the reader to realize the character of the countries represented and of their peoples and purposes in the war.

1916

Central Europe in 1915

The Balkans in 1915

THE WAR IN EASTERN EUROPE

One

THE COUNTRY OF DEATH

We rubbed ourselves from head to foot with camphorated oil, put kerosene on our hair, filled our pockets with moth-balls, and sprinkled naphthaline through our baggage; and boarded a train so saturated with formalin that our eyes and lungs burned as with quicklime. The Americans from the Standard Oil office in Salonika strolled down to bid us a last farewell.

'Too bad,' said Wiley. 'So young, too. Do you want the remains shipped home, or shall we have you buried up there?'

These were the ordinary precautions of travellers bound for Serbia, the country of the typhus – abdominal typhus, recurrent fever, and the mysterious and violent spotted fever, which kills fifty per cent of its victims, and whose bacillus no man had then discovered. Most doctors thought it was carried by clothing lice, but the British R.A.M.C. lieutenant who travelled with us was sceptical.

'I've been up there three months,' he said, 'and I've long ago stopped taking any precautionary measures whatever except a daily bath. As for the lice – one gets used to spending a quiet evening picking them off one.' He snorted at the naphthaline. 'They're really quite fond of it, you know. The truth about the typhus is that no one knows anything about it at all, except that about one-sixth of the Serbian nation is dead of it....'

Already the warm weather and the cessation of the spring rains had begun to check the epidemic – and the virus was weaker. Now there were only a hundred thousand sick in all Serbia, and only a thousand deaths a day – besides cases of the dreadful post-typhus gangrene. In February it must have been ghastly – hundreds dying and delirious in the mud of the streets for want of hospitals.

The foreign medical missions had suffered heavily. Half a hundred priests succumbed after giving absolution to the dying. Out of the four hundred odd doctors with which the Serbian army began the war, less than two hundred were left. And the typhus was not all. Smallpox, scarlet fever, scarlatina, diphtheria raged along the great roads and in far villages, and already there were cases of cholera, which was sure to spread with the coming of the summer in that devastated land; where battle-fields, villages, and roads stank with the lightly buried dead, and the streams were polluted with the bodies of men and horses.

Our lieutenant belonged to the British Army Medical Mission, sent to fight the cholera. He was dressed in full service uniform, and carried a huge sword which got between his legs and embarrassed him frightfully.

'I don't know what to do with the bally thing,' he cried, hurling it into a corner. 'We don't wear swords in the army any more. But we have to out here, because the Serbians won't believe you're an officer unless you carry a sword....'

As we crawled slowly up between barren hills along the yellow torrent of the Vardar, he told us how the English had persuaded the Serbian Government to stop all train service for a month, in order to prevent the spread of disease; then they ordered sanitary improvements in the filthy towns, compelled anti-cholera vaccination, and began to disinfect whole sections of the population. The Serbians sneered – these English were evidently cowards. When Colonel Hunter, unable to secure decent quarters, threatened the authorities that if one of his men died of typhus he would abandon Serbia, a storm of irony burst. Colonel Hunter was a coward!

4

And the Americans were cowards, too, when, with half their units infected, they abandoned Gievgieli. To the Serbians, the taking of preventive measures was a proof of timidity. They regarded the immense ravages of the epidemic with a sort of gloomy pride – as mediæval Europe regarded the Black Death.

The gorge of the Vardar, as if it were a sterile frontier between Greek Macedonia and the high valleys of New Serbia, broadened out into a wide valley rimmed with stony hills, beyond which lay mountains still higher, with an occasional glimpse of an abrupt snow peak. From every canyon burst rapid mountain streams. In this valley the air was hot and moist; irrigation ditches, lined with great willows, struck off from the river, across fields of young tobacco-plants, acres upon acres of mulberry-trees, and ploughed land of heavy, rich clay that looked like cotton country. Here every field, every shelf of earth, was cultivated. Higher up, on bare slopes among the rocks, sheep and goats pastured, tended by bearded peasants with huge crooks, clad in sheepskin coats, spinning wool and silk on wooden distaffs. Irregular, white, red-roofed villages meandered along rutted spaces where squat little oxen and black water-buffaloes dragged creaking carts. Here and there was the galleried *konak* of some wealthy Turk of the old régime, set in yellow-green towering willows, or flowering almond-trees heavy with scent; and over the tumbled little town a slender grey minaret, or the dome of a Greek church.

All sorts of people hung about the stations – men turbaned and fezzed and capped with conical hats of brown fur, men in Turkish trousers, or in long shirts and tights of creamy homespun linen, their leather vests richly worked in coloured wheels and flowers, or in suits of heavy brown wool ornamented with patterns of black braid, high red sashes wound round and round their waists, leather sandals sewed to a circular spout on the toe and bound to the calf with leather ribbons wound to the knees; women with the Turkish *yashmak* and bloomers, or in leather and woollen jackets embroidered in bright colours, waists of the raw silk they weave in the villages, embroidered linen underskirts, black aprons worked in flowers, heavy overskirts woven in vivid bars of colour and caught up behind, and yellow or white silk kerchiefs on their heads. Many wore a black kerchief – the only sign of mourning. And always and everywhere gypsies – the men in a kind of bright turban, the women with gold pieces for earrings and patches and scraps of gay rags for dresses, barefooted – shuffling along the roads beside their caravans, or lounging about the rakish black tents of their camps.

A tall, bearded man in black introduced himself in French as a Serbian secret-service officer whose job was to keep us under observation. Once a dapper young officer came aboard and questioned him, nodding to us. The other responded.

'*Dobra!* Good!' he said, clicking his heels and saluting.

'That station,' remarked the secret-service man as the train moved on again, 'is the frontier. We are now in Serbia.'

We caught a glimpse of several big, gaunt men lounging on the platforms, rifles with fixed bayonets slung at their shoulders, without any uniform except the soldiers *kepi*.

'What would you?' shrugged our friend, smiling. 'We Serbians have no longer any uniforms. We have fought four wars in three years – the First and Second Balkan Wars, the Albanian revolt, and now this one.... For three years our soldiers have not changed their clothes.'

Now we were passing along a narrow field planted with small wooden crosses, that might have been vine poles, spaced about three feet apart; they marched beside the train for five minutes.

'The typhus cemetery of Gievgieli,' he said laconically. There must have been thousands of those little crosses, and each marked a grave!

There came in sight a great, tramped-down space on a

hillside beyond, honeycombed with burrows leading into the brown earth, and humped into round hutches of heaped-up mud. Men crawled in and out of the holes, ragged, dirty fellows in every variety of half-uniform, with rifle-belts criss-crossed over their breasts like Mexican revolutionists. Between were stacked rifles, and there were cannon with ox-yoke limbers and half a hundred springless ox-carts ranged along the side, while farther on the hobbled oxen grazed. Below the mud huts, at the bottom of the hill, men were drinking from the yellow river that poured down from a score of infected villages up the valley. Around a fire squatted twenty or more, watching the carcass of a sheep turn in the flames.

'This regiment has come to guard the frontier,' explained our friend. 'It was here that the Bulgarian *comitadjis* tried to break through and cut the railroad last week. At any moment they might come again.... Is the Bulgarian Government responsible, or did the Austrians pay them? One can never tell, in the Balkans.'

And now, every quarter mile we passed a rude hut made of mud and twigs, before which stood a ragged, hollow-cheeked soldier, filthy and starved-looking, but with his rifle at present arms. All over Serbia one saw these men – the last desperate gleaning of the country's manhood – who live in the mud, with scanty food and miserable clothing, guarding the long-deserted railroad tracks.

At first there seemed no difference between this country and Greek Macedonia. The same villages, a little more unkempt – tiles gone from the roofs, white paint chipped from the walls; the same people, but fewer of them, and those mostly women, old men, and children. But soon things began to strike one. The mulberry-trees were neglected, the tobacco-plants were last year's, rotting yellow; corn-stalks stood spikily in weedy fields unturned for twelve months or more. In Greek Macedonia, every foot of arable land was worked; here only one field out of ten showed signs of cultivation.

Occasionally we saw two oxen, led by a woman in bright yellow head-dress and brilliantly coloured skirt, dragging a wooden plough carved from a twisted oak limb, which a soldier guided, his rifle slung from his shoulder.

The secret-service man pointed to them. 'All the men of Serbia are in the army – or dead – and all the oxen were taken by the government to draw the cannon and the trains. But since December, when we drove the Austrians out, there has been no fighting. So the government sends the soldiers and the oxen over Serbia, wherever they are wanted, to help with the ploughing.'

Sometimes, in details like these, there flashed before our imaginations a picture of this country of the dead: with two bloody wars that swept away the flower of its youth, a two months' hard guerilla campaign, then this fearful struggle with the greatest military power on earth, and a devastating plague on top of that. Yet from the ruins of a whole people, imperial ambitions were already springing, which might one day threaten all southern Europe.

Gievgieli shares with Valievo the distinction of being the worst plague-spot in Serbia. Trees, station, and buildings were splashed and spattered with chloride of lime, and armed sentries stood guard at the fence, where a hundred ragged people pressed murmuring – for Gievgieli was quarantined. We stared through the fence at a wide, rough street of cobbles and mud, flanked by one-storey buildings white with disinfectant; at almost every door flapped a black flag, the sign of death in the house.

A stout, mustached man in a dirty collar, spotted clothing, and a smutty Panama pulled down over his eyes stood on the platform, surrounded by a dense circle of soldiers. He held a small wild flower on high, and addressed the secret-service man volubly and excitedly.

'See!' he cried. 'This flower I found in that field beyond the river. It is very curious! I do not know this flower! It is evidently of the family of the *orchidæ!*' He scowled and fixed the secret-service man with a menacing eye. 'It is not of the family of the *orchidæ?*'

'It has certain characteristics, indeed,' said the other timidly. 'This tongue.... But the pistil –'

The fat man shook the flower. 'Nonsense! It is of the family of the *orchidæ!*'

The soldiers round about broke into a hum of argument: '*Da! Orchida!*' '*Ne je orchida!*' 'But it is evidently an orchid!' 'What do *you* know of orchids, George Georgevitch? At Ralya, where you come from, they haven't even grass!' There was a laugh at this. Above it rose the fat man's voice, insistent, passionate: 'I tell you it is an orchid! It is a new kind of orchid! It is unknown to the science of botany –'

Robinson caught the infection of the argument. 'Orchid?' he said to me with a sneer. 'Of course it's not an orchid!'

'It *is* an orchid!' I returned hotly. 'It is formed very like the lady's-slippers that we see in American woods –'

The fat man wheeled around and erupted into broken English, glaring at us. 'Yes, yes!' he said eagerly. 'The same. Are you Americans? I have been in America. I have tramped through Kansas and Missouri, working on the farms of wheat. I have walked through the Panhan'le of Texas, with work at the cattle-ranch. I am on foot gone through Seattle to San Francisco, to Sacramento, crossing the Sierras and the desert to Yuma in Arizona – you know Yuma? No? I am studying all kind of farming from first-hand for to apply these experiences to Serbian farms. My name is Lazar Obichan. I am an Agro-Geolog, and secretary in Department of Agriculture in government at Belgrade. Yes.' He cleared his throat, waved his elbows to make a space in the crowd, and seized us each by a lapel.

'I am sent here to study soil, climate, and crop conditions of New Serbia. I am an expert. I have invented a new method to tell what can be grown in any soil, in any country. It is automatic, simple, can be appli' by anybody – a new science. Listen! You give me the humidity – I put her *there*.' He poked Robinson stiffly in the shoulder-blade. 'Then you give me the mean temperatoor – I put him *there*.' A jab near Robinson's kidney. 'From humidity I draw a vertical line straight down, isn't it? From mean temperatoor I draw horizontal line straight across.' He suited the action to the word, furrowing the artist's diaphragm. His voice rose. 'Until the two lines meet! And the point where they meet, there is the figure which gives the evaporation for one day!' He poked us sim- ultaneously in the chest to emphasize each word, and repeated: 'The Evaporation for One Day!' He threw both hands up and beamed upon us, pausing to allow this to sink in. We were impressed.

'But that is not all I have in my mind,' he went on heavily. 'There is a vast commercial and financial scheme – immense! Listen! After this war Serbia she will need much money, much foreign capitals. From where will he come? From England? No. England will need all at home. France and Russia will be absolute exhausticated. No capitals from Europe. Where then? I tell you. From America. America is rich. I have been in her and I know how rich. Listen! We will establish a Serbian-American Bank with American capitals and American managers. It will sit in Belgrade. It will lend money to Ser- bians – big profit! Serbian law allows to charge twelve per cent interest – twelve per cent! It will loan to farmers at big interest. It will buy land from poor people, split up in small pieces and sell back at four hundred per cent profit. Serbians poor now, will sell land cheap – but Serbians need land, must have land. We are bankrupted here now – you can buy – how do you say? – you can buy all Serbia for a music! Then these bank, she will open in Belgrade a permanent exhibition of American products and take orders – American shoes, Amer- ican machines, American cloth – and in New York she will open one of Serbian products and take orders. Make money –

big! You shall write about in your papers. If you have capitals put in these bank!'

On the station a bell was ringing. The station master blew a horn, the engine whistled, the train began to move. We tore our lapels from Mr Obichan's thumbs and ran. He raced along with us, still talking.

'Serbia is very rich country in natural resources,' he shouted. 'Here there is soil for cotton, tobacco, silk – very fine alluvial lands. Southern slopes of hills for vineyards! Farther up in mountains wheat, plums, peaches, apples. In the Machva prunes –' We swung on board. 'Minerals –' he yelled after us. 'Gold – copper – Labour cheap –' And then we lost his voice. Later on we asked a Serbian official about him.

'Lazar Obichan?' he said. 'Yes, we know him. He is under observation – suspected of selling military secrets to the Austrian Government!'

Late in the afternoon we halted on a siding to let a military train pass – twelve open flat cars packed with soldiers, in odds and ends of uniforms, wrapped in clashing and vividly coloured blankets. It had begun to rain a little. A gypsy fiddler played wildly, holding his one-stringed violin before him by the throat, which was carved rudely to represent a horse's head; and about him lay the soldiers, singing the newest ballad of the Austrian defeat:

> 'The Swabos* came all the way to Ralya,
> But no further came they –
> Hey, *Kako to?*
> Yoy, *Sashto to?*

> 'They won't soon forget Rashko Pol,
> For there they met the Serbs!
> Hey, how was that?
> Yoy, why was that?

* Swabos – Austrians.

'And now the Swabos know
How the Serbs receive intruders!
  Hey, *Tako to!*
  Yoy, *that* was how!'

Every regiment has two or three gypsies, who march with the troops, playing the Serbian fiddle or the bagpipes, and accompany the songs that are composed incessantly by the soldiers – love-songs, celebrations of victory, epic chants. And all through Serbia they are the musicians of the people, travelling from one country festa to another, playing for dancing and singing. Strange substitution! The gypsies have practically replaced the old-time travelling bards, the *goosslari*, who transmitted from generation to generation through the far mountain valleys the ancient national epics and ballads. And yet they alone in Serbia have no vote. They have no homes, no villages, no land – only their tents and their dilapidated caravans.

We tossed some packages of cigarettes among the soldiers in the cars. For a moment they didn't seem to understand. They turned them over and over, opened them, stared at us with heavy, slow, flat faces. Then light broke – they smiled, nodding to us. '*Fala*,' they said gently. '*Fala lepo!* Thanks beautifully!'

Two

THE WAR CAPITAL

Nish. We took a tumble-down cab – whose bottom-board immediately fell out – attached to two dying horses and driven by a bandit in a high fur cap, and jolted up a wide street paved with mud and wide-set sharp cobbles. Round about the city the green hills rose, beautiful with new leaves and with every flowering fruit-tree, and over the wide-flung Turkish roofs, and the few mean plaster buildings in the European style, loomed the bulbous Greek domes of the cathedral. Here and there was the slender spire of a minaret, crisscrossed with telephone-wires. The street opened into a vast square, a sea of mud and cobbles bounded by wretched huts, across which marched steel poles carrying hundreds of wires and huge modern arc-lights. At one side an ox lay on his back, feet clewed up to a wooden beam, while peasants shod him with solid iron plates, as they had done it for half a thousand years.

Austrian prisoners in uniform wandered freely everywhere, without a guard. Some drove wagons, others dug ditches, and hundreds loitered up and down in idleness. We learned that by paying fifty *denars* to the government, you could have one for a servant. All the legations and consulates were manned with them. And the prisoners were glad to be servants, for there was no decent place for them to live, and scant food. Now and then an Austrian officer passed along, in full uniform and with his sword.

'Escape?' said one government official we interrogated. 'No, they do not try. The roads are metres deep in mud, the villages are depopulated and full of disease, there is no food. . . . It is difficult enough to travel by train in Serbia – on foot it would be impossible. And there are the guards all along the frontier. . . .'

We passed a big hospital where pale prisoners leaned from the windows upon dirty blankets, dragged themselves in and out of the doors, and lay propped up on piles of drying mud along the road. These were only survivors; for out of the sixty thousand Austrians captured in the war, twelve thousand were already dead of typhus.

Beyond the square was the street again, between rough one-storey houses, and we were in the market-place. A dull roar rose from the haggling of hundreds of peasants in ten different national costumes – homespun linen embroidered with flowers, high fur hats, fezzes, turbans, and infinite varieties and modifications of Turkish trousers. Pigs squealed, hens squawked; underfoot were heaped baskets of eggs and herbs and vegetables and red peppers; majestic old men in sheep-skins shuffled along with lambs in their arms. Here was the centre of the town. There were two or three restaurants and foul-smelling cafés, the dingy Hotel Orient, the inevitable American shoe-store, and amid cheap little shops, sudden windows ablaze with expensive jewellery and extravagant women's hats.

Along the sidewalks elbowed a multitude of strangely assorted people: gypsies, poverty-stricken peasants, gen-darmes with great swords, in red and blue uniforms, tax-collectors dressed like generals, also with swords, smart army officers hung with medals, soldiers in filthy tatters, their feet bound with rags – soldiers limping, staggering on crutches, without arms, without legs, discharged from the overcrowded hospitals still blue and shaking from the typhus – and every-where the Austrian prisoners. Government officials hurried by with portfolios under their arms. Fat Jewish army contractors hobnobbed with political hangers-on over maculate café tables. Women government clerks, wives and mistresses of officers, society ladies, shouldered the peasant women in their humped-up gay skirts and high-coloured socks. The government from Belgrade had taken refuge in Nish, and a mountain village of twenty thousand inhabitants had become a city of one hundred and twenty thousand – not counting those who had died.

For the typhus had swept the town, where people were living six and ten in a room, until everywhere the black flags flapped in long, sinister vistas, and the windows of the cafés were plastered with black paper death-notices.

We crossed the muddy Nishava River on the bridge which leads to the heavy, arabesqued gate of the ancient Turkish citadel, which was Roman before the Turks, and where Constantine the Great was born. On the grass along the foot of the great wall sprawled hundreds of soldiers, sleeping, scratching themselves, stripping and searching their bodies for lice, tossing and twisting in fever. Everywhere about Nish, wherever there was a spot of worn grass, the miserable people clustered, picking vermin from each other.

The stench of the city was appalling. In the side streets open sewers trickled down among the cobbles. Some sanitary measures had been taken – such as the closing of cafés and restaurants from two o'clock until six every day in order to disinfect them – but still it was an even chance of typhus if you stayed in a hotel or public building. Luckily the hospitable American vice-consul, Mr Young, took us in at the consulate and introduced us at the Diplomatic Club, which had dining-rooms over an abandoned restaurant, and where good food was to be got when half the town was starving. The entrance was through a pigsty, after stepping across an open sewer; and when you opened the club-room door, your astonished eyes encountered tables, decorated with flowers and covered with silver and snowy linen, and a head waiter in smart evening dress, an Austrian prisoner by the name of Fritz, who had been head waiter at the Carlton in London before the war. To see the British minister sail majestically past the pigsty and mount the club stairs as if it were Piccadilly was a thing worth coming miles for.

Such was Nish, as we first saw it. Two weeks later we returned, after the rains had altogether ceased, and the hot sun had dried the streets. It was a few days after the feast of St George, which marks the coming of the spring in Serbia. On that day all Serbia rises at dawn and goes out into the woods and fields, gathering flowers and dancing and singing and feasting all day. And even here, in this filthy, overcrowded town, with the tragic sadness of war and pestilence over every house, the streets were a gay sight. The men peasants had changed their dirty heavy woollens and sheepskins for the summer suit of embroidered dazzling linen. All the women wore new dresses and new silk kerchiefs, decorated with knots of ribbon, with leaves and flowers – even the ox-yokes and the oxen's heads were bound with purple lilac branches. Through the streets raced mad young gypsy girls in Turkish trousers of extravagant and gorgeous colours, their bodices gleaming with gold braid, gold coins hung in their ears. And I remember five great strapping women with mattocks over their shoulders, who marched singing down the middle of the road to take their dead men's places in the work of the fields.

We were received by Colonel Soubotitch, chief of the Red Cross, in his headquarters. He described the terrible lack of all medical necessities in Serbia, and painted us a graphic picture of people dying in the streets of Nish only a month before. I noticed a handsome peasant blanket on his bed.

'My mother wove that for me,' he said simply, 'in the village where I live. She is a peasant. We are all peasants in Serbia – that is our pride. Voyvoda Putnik, commander-in-chief of the army, is a poor man; his father was a peasant. Voyvoda Michitch, who won the great battle that hurled the Austrian army from our country, is a peasant. Many of the deputies to the Skouptchina, our parliament, are peasants, who sit there in peasant dress.' He stared at the bed. 'And on that bed, on that very blanket which you so admired, I stood here where I now stand and watched my son die of typhus, two months ago. What will you? We must do our duty....'

He threw back his shoulders with a visible effort. 'So you want to see a typhus hospital? Ah, they are not interesting now. The worst is over. But I will give you a letter to Stanoievitch, at Chere Kula.'

We drove to Chere Kula, a mile out of town, late one sombre afternoon in the pouring rain. The name is Turkish, meaning 'Mound of Skulls'; it is literally a tower of skulls of Serbian warriors, erected near the site of a great battle fought more than a century ago, as a monument to the Turkish victory. Lieutenant Stanoievitch, in command of the hospital, unlocked the Greek chapel which the Serbians have built over the holy spot. In the dim light it loomed there, completely filling the chapel, a great round tower of clay with a few grinning heads still embedded in it, and draped with wreaths of faded flowers.

Around this sinister memorial were grouped the brick buildings of the typhus hospital, and the wooden barracks where the overflow was lodged. The wind set our way, carrying the stench of bodies sweating with fever, of sick men eating, of the rotting of flesh. We entered a barrack, along whose walls cots lay touching each other, and in the feeble light of two lanterns we could see the patients writhing in their dirty blankets, five and six crowded into two beds. Some sat up, apathetically eating; others lay like the dead; still others gave short, grunting moans, or shouted suddenly in the grip of delirium. The hospital orderlies, who slept in the same room, were all Austrian prisoners.

'I have been put in charge of this hospital only three days,' said the lieutenant. 'Before I came it was pretty bad. Now we have only twenty deaths a day. There are eight hundred patients – you see, we have no room for even these.'

We passed through fetid ward after fetid ward, smelling of decomposition and death, until we were wrung with the helplessness of these big men, and our stomachs were turned with the stench.

Later, we dined with Stanoievitch and his staff of young doctors and medical students. The good red wine of the country went around, and in a gay and lively argument about the war we forgot for a moment the poor devils dying on the other side of the wall. Stanoievitch, flushed with wine, was boasting of how the Serbians had smashed the Austrian army.

'What are these French and English doing?' he cried impatiently. 'Why do they not beat the Germans? What they need there are a few Serbians to show them how to make war. We Serbians know that all that is needed is the willingness to die – and the war would soon be over ...!'

Three

TOWARD THE FRONT

Next morning early we were on our way to Kraguijevatz, the army headquarters. Our train was loaded with ammunition and American flour for the army at the front, and we carried five cars full of soldiers, in sheepskins, peasant dress, and Austrian uniforms picked up in the rout of December – one man even wore a German casque. They sang an interminable ballad to a minor air, about how old King Peter went to the trenches during the battle of Kolubara River:

> 'Kral Peter rose from his bed one morning
> And said to his dearly beloved son, Prince Alexander,
> "O brave, courageous Prince, my son
> Who leads so well the army of Serbia,
> The Swabos have passed Kroupaign, –
> Their powerful hosts, like the rushing Morava,
> Have passed Valievo....
> I shall go forth to conquer or to die with them!"
> He girt upon him his bright sword....'

The railway line paralleled the Morava River. Here all was green, and in the black loam of the fields women were ploughing with oxen, and winding wool on distaffs as they ploughed. White, low, tiled houses, their balconies overhung with graceful Turkish arches, their corners painted in coloured lozenges, lay hidden amid plum and apple trees in bloom. Beyond them stretched meadows under water, where thousands of frogs made a gigantic croaking chorus, audible above the roaring of the train – for the Morava was in flood. We passed Teshitza, Bagrdan, Dedrevatz, Lapovo, smelling of formalin and spattered with sinister white – pest-holes all.

At Kraguijevatz we were met by a delegate from the Press Bureau, erstwhile lecturer on comparative literature at the University of Belgrade. He was a large-featured, absent-minded young man with fat knees incased in pearl riding-breeches, a bright-green felt hat over one ear, and a naughty twinkle in his eye. Within two hours we were calling him 'Johnson,' which is a literal translation of his name.

Johnson knew every one, and every one knew him. He kept up a running scandalous comment on the people that we passed, and would halt the cab for long periods while he got out and exchanged the latest spicy gossip with some friend. Finally, we would shout to him: 'For Heaven's sake, Johnson, hurry up!'

'Excuse me, sair!' he would respond solemnly. 'You must have patience. Thees is war-time!'

We found the chief of the Press Bureau, former professor of public law at the University of Belgrade, hard at work reading a novel of George Meredith. Johnson explained that the Press Bureau was a very important and active organization.

'We make here many jokes about prominent people, epigrams, and rhymes. For instance, one of the conspirators in the assassination of the Archduke Ferdinand was an officer of the Serbian army during the retreat. He feared that he would be recognized if taken prisoner, so he shaved his beard. In the Press Bureau we have made a sonnet about him, in which we said that it was in vain to shave his beard when he could not shave his prominent nose! Yes, sair. In the Press Bureau we make sometimes two hundred sonnets a day.'

Johnson was a dramatist of note. He had transplanted to

the Serbian stage the *Comédie Rosse* of the Théâtre Antoine, and had been ostracized by respectable society. 'Because,' he explained, 'my play was obscene. But it was true to Serbian life, and that is the ideal of art, don't you think?'

Johnson was saturated with European culture, European smartness, cynicism, modernism; yet scratch the surface and you found the Serb; the strong, virile stock of a young race not far removed from the half-savagery of a mountain peasantry, intensely patriotic and intensely independent.

But many Serbian 'intellectuals' are like the city of Belgrade, where only three years ago the peasants drove their creaking ox-carts along unpaved streets deep in mud, between one-storey houses like the houses of Nish – and which now puts on the buildings, the pavements, the airs and vices of Paris and Vienna. They affect modern art, modern music, the tango and fox-trot. They ridicule the songs and costumes of the peasants.

Sometimes these affectations are laughable. We rode during all one day on horseback over the battle-field of Gouchevo Mountain with a young officer – also of the university faculty – who had lived for three years the life of a fighting nomad, such as no Englishman, Frenchman, or German could have endured. He had gone through the terrible retreat, and still more terrible attack of that winter campaign, sleeping out in the rain or in huts full of vermin, eating the coarse food of the peasants or no food, and thriving on it.

'I am so fond of the country,' he said as we rode along. 'It is so pastoral, don't you think? I am always reminded of Beethoven's Pastoral Symphony when I am in the country.' He whistled a few bars abstractedly. 'No, I made a mistake. That is the Third, isn't it?'

We discovered afterward that his father was a peasant, and all his forebears since the Serbs first came down from the plains of Hungary had been peasants, and had lived in this 'country' which reminded him only of Beethoven!

And in Serbia they are still sensitive about Shaw's 'Arms and the Man.' . . .

We dined at the general staff mess, in the rude throne-room of the palace of Milan Obrenovitch, first of the Serbian kings; his gaudy red-plush-and-gilt throne still stands there, and on the walls are pictures of Milosh Obilich and the other heroes of Serbia's stormy history, and of the Serbian *comitadji* leaders who died by the hands of the Turks in Macedonia in the years before the Balkan War.

'This palace is one of our oldest national monuments,' said Johnson. 'It was built more than fifty years ago.'

Astonishing, the youth of the kingdom of Serbia. Less than a hundred years have passed since she emerged as a free state from five centuries of Turkish domination – and in that time what a history she has had!

The secret dream of every Serb is the uniting of all Serbian people in one great empire: Hungarian Croatia, identical in race and spoken language – Dalmatia, home of Serbian literature – Bosnia, fountain-head of Serbian poetry and song – Montenegro, Herzegovina, and Slovenia. An empire fifteen millions strong, reaching from Bulgaria to the Adriatic, and from Trieste, east and north, far into the plains of Hungary, which will liberate the energies of the fighting, administrative people of the kingdom of Serbia, penned in their narrow mountain valleys, to the exploitation of the rich plains country, and the powerful life of ships at sea.

Every peasant soldier knows what he is fighting for. When he was a baby, his mother greeted him, 'Hail, little avenger of Kossovo!' (At the battle of Kossovo, in the fourteenth century, Serbia fell under the Turks.) When he had done something wrong, his mother reproved him thus: 'Not that way will you deliver Macedonia!' The ceremony of passing from infancy to boyhood was marked by the recitation of an ancient poem:

'Ja sam Serbin,'

it began,

'I am a Serbian, born to be a soldier,
Son of Iliya, of Milosh, of Vasa, of Marko.'

(National heroes, whose exploits here followed at length)

'My brothers are numerous as grapes in the vineyard,
But they are less fortunate than I, a son of a free Serbia!
Therefore must I grow quickly, learn to sing and shoot,
That I may hasten to help those who wait for me!'

And in the Serbian schools the children are taught not only the geography of old Serbia, but of all the Serbian lands, *in the order of their redemption* – first Macedonia, then Dalmatia, Bosnia, Herzegovina, Croatia, Banat, and Batchka!

Now Kossovo is avenged and Macedonia delivered, within the lifetime of these soldiers who listened to their mothers and never forgot their 'brothers, numerous as grapes in the vineyard.' But even while we were in Serbia, other complications threatened.

'What if Italy takes Dalmatia?' I asked a government official.

'It is very exasperating,' he replied, 'for it means that after we have recovered from this war we must fight again!'

An old officer that we met later said, with a sort of holy enthusiasm: 'We thought that this dream of a great Serbia would come true – but many years in the future, many years. And here it is realized in our time! This is something to die for!'

And the boy who sang 'Son of Free Serbia' has made his country one of the most democratic in the world. It is governed by the Skouptchina, a one-chamber parliament elected by universal suffrage and proportional representation – the Senate, derisively known as the 'Museum,' was abolished in 1903. King Alexander tried to rule autocratically, and they murdered him; the present King is strictly a figurehead, limited by a liberal constitution. There is no aristocracy in Serbia. Only the King's brother and the King's sons are princes, and to the Crown Prince Regent the ultra-democrats and Socialists refuse even that title, referring to him always as the 'Manifest-Signer.' Queen Draga attempted to establish an order of nobility, 'but,' as Johnson said, laughing, 'we keeled her!'

The great landlords of Rumania are unknown in Serbia. Here every peasant has a right to five acres of land, inalienable for debt or taxes; he joins fields with his sons and daughters and nephews and nieces, until all through Serbia there exist co-operative estates known as *zadrougas*, where generations of one family, with its ramifications, live together in communal ownership of all their property. And as yet there is no industrial population in Serbia, and few rich men.

That night we heard the dramatic story of the great Serbian victory of December. Twice the Austrians invaded the country, and twice were hurled back, and the streets of Valievo groaned with wounded lying in the rain. But the second time the enemy held Shabatz, Losnitza, and the two rich provinces of Machva and Podrigna, and the heights of Gouchevo. The Serbians could not dislodge them from their strongly intrenched positions. And then, in the bitter weather of December, the Austrians began the third invasion with five hundred thousand men against two hundred and fifty thousand. Pouring across the frontier at three widely separated points, they broke the Serbian lines and rolled the little army back among its mountains. Belgrade was abandoned to the enemy. Twice the Serbians made a desperate stand, and twice they were forced to fall back. Ammunition began to fail – the cannon had less than twenty shells apiece. The enemy passed Krupaign and Valievo and was within forty-five miles of Kraguijevatz, headquarters of the Serbian general staff.

And then, at the last minute, something happened. New supplies of ammunition arrived from Salonika, and the younger officers revolted against their more cautious elders, shouting that it was as well to die attacking as to be slaughtered in the trenches. General Michitch ordered an offensive. The beaten Serbians, rushing from their trenches, fell upon the leisurely Austrian columns coming along narrow mountain defiles to attack. Caught on the march, burdened with big guns and heavy baggage-trains on roads almost impassable from mud, the Austrians resisted furiously, but were forced to recoil. The line was broken. Their centre, smashed by Michitch and the first army, broke and fled in panic across the country, abandoning baggage, ammunition, and guns, and leaving behind thousands of dead and wounded, and hospitals crammed with men raving with typhus. This is how the typhus, beginning somewhere up in the plains of Hungary, entered Serbia with the Austrian army. For a time the left wing tried to hold Belgrade, but the exultant, ragged Serbians drove them literally into the River Save and shot them as they swam across.

This great battle, which Voyvoda Michitch reported laconically with the proud telegram, 'There remain no Austrian soldiers on Serbian soil except prisoners,' has been given no name. Some call it the Battle of Kolubara River and others the Battle of Valievo. But it is, perhaps, the most wonderful feat of arms in all the great World War.

At the right hand of the colonel sat a pope in the long black robes of the Greek Church. He was not unctuous and sly like the Greeks, however – a great ruddy man who laughed uproariously and drank his wine with the officers. These Serbian priests are remarkable people. They are the teachers, the transmitters of patriotism among the peasants. They are elected to the Skouptchina as deputies of districts.

'Why not?' he said in French. 'In Serbia there is no Clerical party. We are all one here – eh?' He turned to the colonel, who nodded. 'I have now been fighting in the army for three years – not as a priest, but as a Serbian soldier. Yes, we are the State Church, but the government also subsidizes the Protestant and Catholic Churches, and even the Moham-medan *hadjis*. Why, it is really extraordinary. The government pays the Mohammedan *mufti* thirty thousand *denars* a year, and the metropolitan of the Serbian Church only gets twenty thousand! Our people do not forget that Milan Obrenovitch proclaimed the revolution against the Turks at a village church, with a pope at his side. We are Serbs and men first, and priests afterward,' He laughed. 'Have you heard the story of how the Serbian bishop, Duchitch, shocked the Bishop of London? No? Well, they dined together in England.'

' "You are fortunate," said the Bishop of London, "in your people. I am told they are very devout."

' "Yes," said Mr Duchitch, "in Serbia we do not trust too much to God. We prayed God five centuries to free us from the Turks, and finally took guns and did it ourselves!" '

It was midnight when we took the train for Belgrade, less than a hundred kilometres away, but by morning we were still far from the city. We crawled slowly along, waiting hours on sidings for the passing of trains going north laden with soldiers and with supplies, and empty trains going south; for we were now within the lines of the Army of the Danube, and on the main military artery serving fifty thousand men. It was a region of high, rolling hills, and here and there a loftier mountain crowned with the ruined castle of some Dahee overlord, dating from the Turkish days. There was no longer any pretence of cultivation. Hillside after hillside hollowed into caves or covered with huts of mud and straw housed the ragged regiments; trenches gashed in the sloping meadows crisscrossed that hard-fought ground – and in spots where the battle had been particularly fierce, the jagged stumps of great oak-trees stood branchless and leafless, stripped bare by the hail of shells and rifle-bullets.

The railway-station of Belgrade had been destroyed in the

bombardment, and one by one the searching Austrian cannon had wrecked the nearer stations, so we were forced to leave the train at Rakovitza, six miles out, and drive to the city. The road wound through a beautiful, fertile valley, with white villas and farmhouses smothered in thick blooming chestnuts. Nearer town we entered the shaded road of an immense park, where in summer the fashionable world of Belgrade comes to show its smartest carriages and its newest gowns. Now the roads were weedy, the lawns dusty and unkempt. A shell had wrecked the summer pavilion. Under the big trees at the edge of an ornamental fountain a troop of cavalry was picketed, and a little farther on the tennis-court had been disembowelled to make emplacements for two French cannon – the French sailors of the gun crew, lying around on the grass, shouted gayly to us.

Our carriage had taken a left-hand road, leading toward the River Save, when suddenly a distant deep booming fell upon our ears. It was like nothing else in the world, the double boom of big cannon, and the shrill flight of shells. And now, nearer at hand, off to the left, other great guns answered. A two-horsed cab, its horses galloping, appeared around a turn ahead, and a fat officer leaned out as he passed us.

'Don't go that way!' he shouted. '*Putzaiyu!* They are firing on the road! The English batteries are replying!'

We turned around and took a long detour that led around to the right. For about a quarter of an hour the far shooting continued – then it ceased. A deep, steady humming had been growing more and more audible for some time, filling all the air. Suddenly there came the heavy, sharp crack of a detonation over our heads. We looked up. There, immeasurably high, gleaming like a pale dragon-fly in the sun, an aeroplane hovered. Her lower planes were painted in concentric circles of red and blue. 'French!' said Johnson. She was already turning slowly toward the east and south. Behind her, not more than a hundred yards it seemed, the white puff of an exploding shrapnel slowly flowered. Even as we looked, another distant gun spoke, and another, and the shells leaped after her as she drifted out of our vision behind the trees.

We crawled up a steep hill and descended the other side along a straight, white, unpaved road. In front of us, perched on a high headland between the Danube and the Save, was Belgrade, the *Beograd* of the Serbians, the White City which was ancient when they first came down from the Hungarian mountains, and yet is one of the youngest of the world's cities. Down at the bottom of the hill a long double file of Austrian prisoners, dusty with the long march from Rakovitza, stood patiently in the sun while two Serbian officers questioned them.

'Of what race are you?'

'I am a Serb from Bosnia, *gospodine*,' answered the prisoner, grinning.

'And you?'

'Kratti (Croat) of the mountains.'

'Well, brothers,' said the officer, 'this is a nice thing for you to be fighting for the Swabos!'

'Ah!' answered the Croat. 'We asked permission to fight with you, but they wouldn't let us.' Every one laughed.

'And what race are you?'

'Italiano from Trieste.'

'Tchek.'

'I am Magyar!' growled a sullen-faced, squat man with a look of hate.

'And you?'

'I am Rumaniass!' (Rumanian), said the last man proudly.

A few hundred yards farther along was a great shed stored with all sorts of provisions, fodder, hay, and grain for the army. Here in the hot sun the Austrian prisoners were sweating at their work of loading ox-carts with sacks of flour, their uniforms, hands, and faces caked with white meal. A sentry with a bayoneted rifle walked up and down in front of them, and as he walked he chanted:

'God bless my grandfather, Vladislav Wenz, who came to settle in Serbia forty years ago. If he hadn't, I would now be packing flour with these prisoners!'

Four

BELGRADE UNDER THE AUSTRIAN GUNS

Our carriage rattled, echoing through silent Belgrade. Grass and weeds pushed between the cobbles, untravelled now for half a year. The sound of guns had entirely ceased. A hot sun glazed down, dazzling on the white walls of the houses, and a little warm wind whirled spirals of white dust from the unpaved roadway; it was hard to imagine that the Austrian big guns dominated us, and that any moment they might bombard the city, as they had a dozen times before. Everywhere were visible the effects of artillery fire. Great holes fifteen feet in diameter gaped in the middle of the street. A shell had smashed the roof of the Military College and exploded within, shattering all the windows; the west wall of the War Office had sloughed down under a concentrated fire of heavy guns; the Italian legation was pitted and scarred by shrapnel, and the flag hung ragged from its broken pole. Doorless private houses, with roofs cascading to the sidewalks, showed window-frames swinging idly askew without a pane of glass. Along that crooked boulevard which is Belgrade's main and the only paved street, the damage was worse. Shells had dropped through the roof of the Royal Palace and gutted the interior. As we passed, a draggled peacock, which had once adorned the Royal Gardens, stood screaming in a ruined window, while a laughing group of soldiers clustered on the sidewalk underneath imitating it. Hardly anything had escaped that hail of fire – houses, sheds, stables, hotels, restaurants, shops, and public buildings – and there were many fresh ruins from the latest bombardment, only ten days before. A five-storey office-building with the two top floors blown off by a 30.5-centimetre shell exhibited a half section of a room – an iron bed hanging perilously in the air, and flowered wall-paper decorated with framed pictures, untouched by the freak of the explosion. The University of Belgrade was only a mass of yawning ruins. The Austrians had made it their special target, for there had been the hot-bed of Pan-Serbian propaganda, and among the students was formed the secret society whose members murdered the Archduke Franz Ferdinand.

We met an officer who belonged to this society – a classmate of the assassin. 'Yes,' he said, 'the government knew. It tried to discourage us, but it could do nothing. Of course the government did not countenance our propaganda.' He grinned and winked. 'But how could it prevent? Our constitution guarantees the freedom of assemblies and organizations. ... We are a free country!'

Johnson was unmoved by the wreck.

'For years we have been cramped and inconvenienced in that old building,' he explained. 'But the University was too poor to build again. Now we shall demand in the terms of peace one of the German universities – libraries, laboratories, and all complete. They have many, and we have only one. We have not yet decided whether to ask for Heidelberg or Bonn....'

Already people were beginning to drift back to the city which they had deserted six months before, at the time of the first bombardment. Every evening, toward sundown, the streets became more and more crowded. A few stores timidly opened, some restaurants, and the cafés where the true Belgradian spends all his time sipping beer and watching the fashionable world pass. Johnson kept up a flow of comment on the people who wait at tables, or went by along the street.

'You see that little, important-looking man with the glasses? He is Mr R –, who is very ambitious and thinks himself a great man. He is editor of an insignificant newspaper called *La Dépêche*, which he published here every day under the bombardment, and imagined himself a great hero. But there is a little song about him which is sung all over Belgrade:

> ' "An Austrian cannon-ball flew through the air.
> It said: 'Now I shall destroy Belgrade, the White
>   City';
> But when it saw that it would hit R –
> It held its nose, crying 'Phoot!' – and went the other
>   way!" '

In the corner a stout, dirty man with the look of a Jewish politician was holding forth to a crown.

'That is S –, editor of the *Mali Journal*. There are three brothers, one of them a trick bicycle-rider. This man and the other brother founded a little paper here which lived by blackmailing prominent people. They were desperately poor. No one would pay the blackmail. So they published every day for two weeks a photograph of the bicycle-rider with his bare legs, bare arms, and medals on his chest, so that some heiress with millions of *denars* would become enamoured of his beautiful physique and marry him!'

We visited the ancient Turkish citadel which crowns the abrupt headland towering over the junction of the Save and the Danube. Here, where the Serbian guns had been placed, the Austrian fire had fallen heaviest; hardly a building but had been literally wrecked. Roads and open spaces were pitted with craters torn by big shells. All the trees were stripped. Between two shattered walls we crawled on our bellies to the edge of the cliff overlooking the river.

'Don't show yourselves,' cautioned the captain who had us in charge. 'Every time the Swabos see anything moving here, they drop us a shell.'

From the edge there was a magnificent view of the muddy

Danube in flood, inundated islands sticking tufts of tree tops above the water, and the wide plains of Hungary drowned in a yellow sea to the horizon. Two miles away, across the Save, the Austrian town of Semlin slept in radiant sunlight. On that low height to the west and south were planted the invisible threatening cannon. And beyond, following southwest the winding Save as far as the eye could see, the blue mountains of Bosnia piled up against the pale sky. Almost immediately below us lay the broken steel spans of the international railway bridge which used to link Constantinople to western Europe – plunging prodigiously from their massive piers into the turbid yellow water. And up-stream still was the half-sunken island of Tzigalnia, where the Serbian advance-guards lay in their trenches and sniped the enemy on another island four hundred yards away across the water. The captain pointed to several black dots lying miles away up the Danube behind the shoulder of Semlin.

'Those are the Austrian monitors,' he said. 'And that low black launch that lies close in to shore down there to the east, she is the English gunboat. Last night she stole up the river and torpedoed an Austrian monitor. We expect the city to be bombarded any minute now. The Austrians usually take it out on Belgrade.'

But the day passed and there was no sign from the enemy, except once when a French aeroplane soared up over the Save. Then white shrapnel cracked over our heads, and long after the biplane had slanted down eastward again, the guns continued to fire, miles astern.

'They have learned their lesson,' said Johnson complacently. 'The last time they bombarded Belgrade, they were answered by the big English, French, and Russian naval guns, which they did not know were here. We bombarded Semlin and silenced two Austrian positions.'

We made the tour of the foreign batteries with the captain

33

next day. The French guns and their marines were posted among trees on the top of a high, wooded hill overlooking the Save. They were served by French marines. Farther along Russian sailors lolled on the grass about their heavy cannon, and on the sloping meadows back of Belgrade lay the British, guarding the channel of the Danube against the Austrian supply-boats which were moored above Semlin, waiting for a chance to slip past down the Danube, with guns and ammunition for the Turks. The Serbian batteries were a queer mixture of ordnance; there were old field-guns made by Creusot in France for the First Balkan War, ancient bronze pieces cast for King Milan in the Turkish War, and all kinds and calibers captured from the Austrians – German field-guns, artillery manufactured in Vienna for the Sultan, ornamented with Turkish symbols, and new cannon ordered by Yuan Shi Kai, their breeches covered with Chinese characters.

Our window looked out over the roofs of the city to the broad current of the Save, and the sinister highland beyond where the enemy's guns were. At night the great Austrian search-light would flare suddenly upon the stream and the city, blinding; sparks would leap and die among the trees of the river islands, and we would hear the pricking rifle-fire where the outposts lay in mud with their feet in the water, and killed each other in the dark. One night the English batteries roared behind the town, and their shells whistled over our heads as they drove back the Austrian monitors who were trying to creep down the river. Then the invisible guns of the highland across the Save spat red; for an hour heavy missiles hurtled through the sky, exploding miles back about the smoking English guns – the ground shook where we stood.

'So you want to visit the trenches,' said the captain. We had driven out a mile or so through the outskirts of the city that lay along the Save, always in sight of the Austrian guns. Our carriages were spaced two hundred yards apart, for two vehicles together would have drawn fire. Where we stood the shore jutted out into the flooded river behind the trees of a submerged island that screened us from the Austrian bank. 'It is not very safe. We must go in a boat and pass three hundred yards of open water commanded by an Austrian cannon.'

The aged launch was supposed to be armoured; a heavy sheet of tin roofed her engine-pit, and thin steel plates leaned against the bulwarks. As soon as we rounded the protecting curtain of trees, the soldier who was pilot, engineer, and crew stood up and shook his fist at the point of land where the Austrian gun lay.

'Oh, cowards and sons of cowards!' he chanted. 'Why do you not fire, Swabo cowards? Does the sight of unarmed Serbians cause your knees to knock together?'

This he kept up until the launch slipped out of range behind Tzigalnia, alongside a huge cargo-scow, painted black and loophooled for rifles. On her bow in large yellow letters, was *Neboysha*, which is Serbian for 'Dreadnought.'

'That is the Serbian navy,' laughed the captain. 'With her we have fought a great battle. In January, one dark night, we filled her full of soldiers and let her float down the river. That is how we captured this island.'

From the *Neboysha* a precarious plank footbridge on floating logs led between half-submerged willow-trees to a narrow strip of land not more than ten feet wide and two hundred yards long. Here the soldiers had dug their rude rifle-pits, and here they lay forward on the muddy embankment, unshaven, unwashed, clothed in rags, and gaunt with scanty, bad food. From head to foot they were the colour of mud, like animals. Many of the trenches were below the flood level, and held water; you could see where, only two days before, the river had risen until it was up to the men's waists. We could not walk along the line of trenches – soldiers poled us up and down in little scows.

A score of shaggy, big men in fur caps, with rifle-belts crossed over their chests and hand bombs slung at their shoulders, were at work under an armed guard, surlily digging trenches. These were *comitadjis*, the captain said – irregular volunteers without uniform, drawn from the half-bandits, half-revolutionists, who had been making desperate guerilla war against Turks, Bulgarians, and Greeks in Macedonia for years.

'They are under arrest,' he explained. 'They refused to dig trenches or work on the roads. "We have come to fight the Swabos," they said, "not to dig ditches. We are warriors, not labourers!"'

Removing our hats, we peered cautiously through the gaps made for the rifles; a similar barren neck of land appeared about four hundred yards away through the tree tops rising from the water – for all this had once been land – where the Austrians lay. A blue peaked cap bobbed cautiously up – the soldier beside me grunted and fired. Almost immediately there was a scattering burst of shots from the enemy. Bullets whined close over our heads, and from the trees green leaves showered down.

Our boatman thrust off from the *Neboysha* and headed the launch up-stream before he rounded into the channel swept by the Austrian artillery, a quarter of a mile away.

'We will go closer,' said he, 'perhaps it will tempt them.'

The clumsy, chugging boat swept clear. He stood up in the stern, cupped his hands, and bellowed a satirical verse that the soldiers sang:

> 'The Emperor Nicholas rides a black horse,
> The Emperor Franz Joseph rides a mule –
> And he put the bridle on the tail instead of the head,
> So now is the end of Austria!'

Hardly had he finished – the boat was within fifty yards of the sheltering island – when a sudden detonation stunned us.

We hit the bottom of the boat with one simultaneous thud just as something screamed three yards over our heads, and the roof of a building on the shore heaved up with a roar, filling the air with whistling fragments of tiles and lead pellets – shrapnel.

'Whoop!' shouted the steersman. 'There's enough black balls to defeat any candidate!'

Now we were behind the sheltering trees. A row-boat full of soldiers put off from the bank, paddling frantically.

'Don't go out there!' cried the captain to them. 'They are firing!'

'That's why we're going!' they cried altogether, like children. 'Perhaps they'll take a shot at us!' They rounded the island with shouts and a prodigious splashing of oars....

Lunch was ready in the ruins of a great sugar factory, where the colonel in command of the island had his headquarters. To get to it, we crossed a bridge of planks laid on a quaking marsh of brown sugar – tons and tons of it, melted when the Austrian shells had set fire to the place.

The colonel, two captains, four lieutenants, a corporal, and two privates sat down with us. In Serbia the silly tradition that familiarity between officers and men destroys discipline apparently does not exist. Many times in restaurants we noticed a private or a non-commissioned officer approach a table where officers sat, salute stiffly, and then shake hands all around and sit down. And here the sergeant who waited on table took his place between us to drink his coffee and was formally introduced.

One of the privates had been secretary of the Serbian National Theatre before the war. He told us that the charter required fifty performances of Shakespeare a season, and that the Serbians preferred *Coriolanus* to all the other plays.

'*Hamlet*,' he said, 'was very popular. But we have not played it here for fifteen years, for the only actor who could do the part died in 1900.'

37

Five

ALONG THE BATTLE-LINE

A thousand feet up two French aeroplanes hummed slowly west, translucent in the clear morning sunlight. Below and to the left lazy shrapnel burst. The sound of the explosions and the humming of the motors drifted down, minutes later. Our carriages crawled up a hill strewn with villas hidden in new verdure and flowering fruit-trees; and, looking back, we had a last view of Belgrade, the White City, on her headland, and the Austrian shore. Then we plunged into a winding, rutted lane that wandered up beneath trees which met overhead – past low, white peasant houses roofed with heavy Turkish tiles, and fields where women in embroidered leather vests and linen skirts tramped the furrows, leading oxen lent by the army, and followed by soldiers who guided the wooden ploughs. Long strips of homespun linen hung from hedge and fence, bleaching in the sun. Except for the soldiers, the country was destitute of men.

We turned inland, along country roads that were little more than tracks – now one could not use the main road along the Save, for it lay directly under the guns of the Austrian trenches, three hundred yards away across the river. Many times the driver lost the way. We forded rapid mountain streams that washed to the wagon-bed, sank to the hubs in muddy sloughs, crept through winding, deep ravines along the dried beds of torrents, and rattled down steep hills through groves of immense oaks, where droves of half-wild pigs fled squealing before the horses. Once we passed three huge tombstones taller than a man, crowned with the carved turbans that ornament the cenotaphs of the *hadjis*. Immense scimitars were chiselled at their base. Johnson asked some peasants about them, but they answered 'Heroes,' and shrugged their shoulders. Farther on was a white stone sarcophagus lying in a hollow of the hill – the Roman tomb that once enclosed it had been broken up and carried away by the peasants, perhaps centuries ago. Then the track led through the middle of an ancient village graveyard, its moss-grown Greek crosses leaning crazily among dense brush. Everywhere along the way new crosses of stone, painted with gold, green and red, stood under little roofs; these, Johnson explained, were the memorials of men of the neighbourhood who had died in unknown places and whose bodies had never been found. Trees and grass and flowers rioted over the hills. Last year's fields were jungles of weeds. Houses with doors ajar and gaping windows lay amid untended vines. Sometimes we bumped down the wide street of a silent country village where old men dragged themselves to their doors to see us pass, and children romped with wolfish sheep-dogs in the dust, and groups of women came home from the fields with mattocks on their shoulders. This was the *rackia* country – where the native plum brandy comes from; immense orchards of prunes and plums sweetened the heavy air.

We stopped at a *mehana* or village inn to eat the lunch we had brought with us – for in all this country there was not enough food even for the inhabitants. In the dim, cool interior, with its rough wooden tables set on the earthen floor, aged peasants with the simplicity of children took off their hats with grave politeness. '*Dobar dan, gospodine!*' they greeted us. 'Good day, sirs! We hope your voyage is pleasant.' The gnarled old proprietor stooped over his earthen oven, making Turkish coffee in brass cups and telling how the Austrians had come.

'A soldier with a rifle and a bayonet came through this door. "I want money," he said; "all you have – quick!" But I answered that I had no money. "You must have money. Are you not an innkeeper?" Still I said I had none; then he thrust at me with his bayonet – here. You see?' He tremblingly lifted his shirt and showed a long gash, yet unhealed.

'Typhus!' Johnson pointed to the fences before the houses on each side of the road. Almost every one was marked with a painted white cross, sometimes two or three. 'Every cross means a case of typhus in the house.' In half a mile I counted more than a hundred. It seemed as if this buoyant, fertile land held nothing but death or the memorials of death.

Late in the afternoon we topped a hill and saw again the wide-spread Save flooding all its valley, and beyond, foothills piling greenly up the Bosnian mountains, range behind range. Here the river made a great bend, and half concealed in the middle of a wooded plain that seemed entirely under water lay red roofs, white swollen towers and thin minarets – Obrenovatz. We drove down the hill and joined the main road, which rose just above the flood level, like a causeway through wastes of water. In the marshes on either side sacred white storks were solemnly fishing. The ground rose a little in a sort of island at the centre of the flooded country; we rattled along the rocky, unpaved street of a white little Serbian town, low houses set in clumps of green, with double windows to keep out the vampires.

They led us with much ceremony to the house of Gaia Matitch, the postmaster, a nervous, slight man with a sweet smile, who welcomed us at his door. His wife stood beside him, fluttered, anxious, and bursting with the importance of entertaining strangers. The entire family waved us before them into their bedroom, which they had ornamented with the whitest linen, the gayest embroideries, and vases full of flowers from the marsh. Two officers from the divisional headquarters stood around racking their brains for things to make us comfortable; a little girl brought plates of apples and preserved plums and candied oranges; soldiers fell on their knees and pulled at our boots, and another stood by the washstand waiting to pour water over our hands; Gaia Matitch himself wandered in and out of the room, a bottle of *rackia* in his hand, offering us a drink, tidying the chairs and tables, shouting shrill, exasperated orders to the servants.

'We are greatly honoured,' he managed to convey, in a mixture of garbled French, German, and English. 'In Serbia it is the highest honour for a stranger to visit one's house.'

This beautiful Serbian hospitality to foreigners we experienced many times. Once, I remember we were in a strange town where for weeks no new supplies had come in, and there was no tobacco. We went to a shop to try to find some cigarettes.

'Cigarettes!' said the shopkeeper, throwing up his hands. 'Cigarettes are worth double their weight in gold.' He looked at us for a moment. 'Are you strangers?' We said we were. Whereupon, he unlocked an iron safe and handed us each a package of cigarettes. 'The charge is nothing,' he said: 'You are foreigners.'

Our friend Matitch, with the tears standing in his eyes, pointed to two photographs on the wall – one of an old man with a white beard, and the other of a young girl.

'This man is my father,' he said. 'He was seventy-seven years old. When the Austrians took Shabatz they sent him to Buda-Pesth as a prisoner of war, and he is dead there in Hungary. As for my sister here, they took her also – and since August I have heard nothing. I know not whether she is living or dead.'

Here we first began to hear of Austrian atrocities along the western frontier. We could not believe them at first; but later, at Belgrade, at Shabatz, at Losnitza, they were repeated again and again, by those who escaped, by the families of those who were dead or in prison, by sworn statements and the Austrian official lists of prisoners sent to the Serbian Red Cross. At the taking of the border towns the Austrians herded the civil population together – women, old men, and children – and drove them into Austria-Hungary as prisoners of war. More than seven hundred were so taken from Belgrade, and fifteen hundred from Shabatz alone. The official war-prisoner lists of the Austrian Government read cynically like this: Ion Touphechitch, age 84; Darinka Antitch (woman), age 23; Georg Georgevitch, age 78; Voyslav Petronievitch, age 12; Maria Wenz, age 69. The Austrian officers said they did this because it was a punitive expedition against the Serbs, and not a war!

At the mess we heard that we must travel by night to Shabatz, for the road led along the river bank within range of the enemy's trenches. So after dinner the entire staff accompanied us back to Matitch's. Much sour native wine had been flowing, and we went arm in arm hooting and singing along the village street. When Matitch heard that we were not going to spend the night in his house, he almost wept.

'Please stay!' he cried, grasping our arms. 'Isn't my house good enough for you? Is there anything you lack?'

At length, with a sigh he thrust us into the dining-room. There we sat, saying farewell, while Matitch and Mrs Matitch brought wine and dried salt beef to make us thirsty. A courteous officer inquired from Johnson how one drank a health in French; but all he could get was '*A votre sentir!*' which he repeated over and over again. We drank Mrs Matitch's health, at which the good woman was furiously embarrassed. We sang American songs to uproarious applause. Some one stuffed Robinson's pockets full of dried beef, which fell out of his clothes for days afterward. It got along toward midnight, and we ought to have started at ten. Of a sudden Matitch rose to his feet. '*Pobratim!*' he shouted, and all the others echoed '*Pobratim!*' 'I now make you my *probatim* – my blood-brother,' said he, glowing with friendliness. 'It is the old Serbian ceremony. Your arm through mine – so!'

One by one we linked elbows and drank thus, and then threw our arms about each other's necks; and embraced loudly on both cheeks. The company roared and pounded on the table. It was done – and to this day we are *pobratim* with Gaia Matitch.

At length we were in the carriages; the drivers snapped their whips, and we were off, to shouts of '*S Bogom!* Farewell! *Laku Noch!* Happy night!'

There was a bright moon. As we passed the outskirts of the village, two silent, armed figures on horseback fell in behind the first carriage, riding along with us till the danger zone was passed. Now we pitched and tossed over rocks or wallowed through deep mud; again the horses were splashing in water that rose to the hubs, where the river-flood covered the road. The drivers cracked their whips no more, nor shouted – they cursed the horses in low tones, for we were now within hearing of the Austrian trenches. No sound was heard except the beat of the horses' hoofs and the creaking of the carriage.

The moon sank slowly. The mounted guards vanished as mysteriously as they had come. Still we rocked on. Gently the wide, starry sky paled to dawn, and eastward, over the great mountains of Tser, where the Serbians broke the first invasion, came the white and silver dawn. Under a grassy hill crowned with an enormous white Greek church wrecked by artillery fire, a hundred ox-carts were scattered in the fields, their drivers sleeping wrapped in blankets of vivid colours, or squatting around early fires that painted their faces red. They were bound for Belgrade, a week's crawling journey away, to bring back food for the starving country where we were going.

Over the mountains leaped the sun, hot and blinding, and we rattled into the streets of Shabatz, between endless rows of smashed and gutted and empty houses, before the town was awake.

A café stood open. We made for it, and ordered coffee. Was there anything to eat? We were ravenous. The woman shook her head. 'In Shabatz there is not even bread.'

'Eggs!' we cried.

Johnson lazily threw up his hands. 'My dear sairs! Excuse me. There is no eggs. Thees is war!'

'But I saw hens up the street,' I insisted. Finally Johnson consented to ask the woman.

'There are no eggs for sale here,' she replied. 'But since the *gospodine* are strangers, we will *give* you some.'

Shabatz had been a rich and important town, metropolis of the wealthiest department in Serbia, Machva, and the centre of a great fruit, wine, wool, and silk trade. It contained twenty-five hundred houses. Some had been destroyed by the guns; twice as many more were wantonly burned, and all of them had been broken into and looted. One walked along miles and miles of streets – every house was gutted. The invaders had taken linen, pictures, children's playthings, furniture – and what was too heavy or cumbersome to move they had wrecked with axes. They had stabled their horses in the bedrooms of fine houses. In private libraries all the books lay scattered in filth on the floor, carefully ripped from their covers. Not simply a few houses had been so treated – *every* house. It was a terrible thing to see.

At the time of the first invasion many people remained in Shabatz, trusting that they would be safe. But the soldiers were loosed like wild beasts in the city, burning, pillaging, raping. We saw the gutted Hôtel d'Europe, and the blackened and mutilated church where three thousand men, women, and children were penned up together without food or water for four days, and then divided into two groups – one sent back to Austria as prisoners of war, the other driven ahead of the army as it marched south against the Serbians. This is not unsupported rumour or hysterical accusation, as it is often in France and Belgium; it is a fact proved by a mass of sworn testimony, by hundreds of people who made that terrible march. We talked with several; one a very old woman who had been forced at the point of the bayonet to go on foot before the troops more than thirty-five miles to Valievo. Her shoes had rotted from her feet – for ten miles she walked barefoot over the stony road.

In the Prefecture we went over hundreds of reports, affi-davits, and photographs, giving names, ages, addresses of the sufferers, and details of the horrible things the Austrians had done. There was one picture taken at the village of Lechnitza, showing more than a hundred women and children chained together, their heads struck off and lying in a separate heap. At Kravitza old men, women, and children were tortured and fiendishly outraged, then butchered. At Yvremovatz fifty people were herded into a cellar and burned alive. Five unde-fended towns were razed to the ground – forty-two villages were sacked, and the greater part of their inhabitants mass-acred. The typhus, brought into the country by the Austrian army, still ran riot through Shabatz and all the region. And here there were no doctors nor hospitals.

To be perfectly fair, let me say that everywhere we were told it was the Hungarians, and not the Austrian Germans, who had committed these atrocities – the Hungarians, who have always been enemies of the Serbs, in Croatia as well as here. The Austrians themselves seem to have behaved fairly well; they paid for what they took and did not bother peace-able civilians.

But the Hungarians reverted to their savage ancestors, the Huns. When they retreated from Shabatz, in December, they gathered together in the courtyard of Gachitch's pharmacy three hundred Serbian soldiers taken prisoners in battle, shot them slowly and then broke their necks. Belgium can show no horrors as black as these .... The cold-blooded fiends who committed them gave as an excuse that the townspeople had harboured *comitadjis* – who, they had been told by their officers, were savage bandits, to be shot on sight. But in all this region there were no *comitadjis*, nor ever had been. In the country they pretended to believe that the Serbian peasant costume was the *comitadji* uniform – and since every civilian, man, woman, and child, wore it, they butchered them all. The slaughter of the prisoners of war had no excuse.

In this once flourishing and pleasant city hardly two hundred people now lived, camping miserably in their ruined houses, without enough to eat. We wandered in the hot sun through deserted streets, past the square where once the great market of all northwest Serbia had been held, and the peasants had gathered in their bright dress from hundreds of kilometres of rich mountain valleys and fertile plains. It was market-day. A few miserable women in rags stood mournfully by their baskets of sickly vegetables. And on the steps of the gutted Prefecture sat a young man whose eyes had been stabbed out by Hungarian bayonets. He was tall and broad-shouldered, with ruddy cheeks – dressed in the dazzling homespun linen of the peasant's summer costume, and in his hat he wore yellow dandelions. He played a melancholy tune upon a horse-headed Serbian fiddle and sang:

'I am sad, for I have lost the sight of the sun and the green fields and the blossoming plum-trees. God's blessing to you who have given me a *grosh* (four cents). Blessing to all who are about to give –'

The prefect pointed to the broken buildings. 'When the

war is finished we shall make a new Shabatz,' he said. 'The government has already ordered that no one shall repair the old ruined houses. They must be rebuilt entirely new.'

Six

A NATION EXTERMINATED

Next morning we boarded the train of the narrow-gauge railroad which taps the richest part of the Machva, and connects the valley of the Drina with the valley of the Save. Four box-cars followed our carriage, crammed with miserable refugees, chiefly women and children – returning to the homes from which they had fled, destitute and on foot, six months ago, before the Austrian scourge. We went slowly along a vast fertile plain, white with fruit orchards in bloom and green with tall grass and new foliage, between uncultivated fields rank with weeds, and past white houses blackened with fire. All this country had been burned, looted, and its people murdered. Not an ox was seen, and for miles not a man. We passed through little towns where grass grew in the streets and not a single human being lived. Sometimes the train would halt to let the refugees descend; they stood there beside the track, all their possessions in sacks over their shoulders, gazing silently at the ruins of their homes....

The prefect came with us, stopping the train for an hour or so at different villages, to show us the sights. So we visited Prnjavor, once a rich little place of three thousand people, now a waste of burned and smashed dwellings. At the station was a tall, rugged old farmer in peasant costume of rough brown wool, who was introduced to us as Mr Samourovitch, deputy to the Skouptchina. He pointed down into a pool of muddy water beside the railroad track, from which emerged the top of a heap of earth, crowned with two wooden crosses.

'That is the grave of my old father and mother,' he said without emotion, 'the Swabos shot them for *comitadjis*.' We walked on into the town, to a place where once a house stood, that now was a black heap of ashes and burnt timbers. 'In this place,' he went on, 'the Hungarians gathered together a hundred citizens of Prnjavor – they could not cram them all into the house, so they made the rest stand close and bound them to it with ropes – and then they set fire to the house, and shot those who tried to escape.... This long, low pile of dirt is their grave.' The story seemed too horrible for any possibility, and I made particular inquiries about it. But it was literally true. Swiss doctors examined the spot and took photographs of the bodies before they were buried; they were all old people, women and children.

Stagnant pools from the recent rains, covered with green slime, stood in the streets. A smell of decaying bodies and neglected filth was in the air. Before almost every house at least one sinister white cross was painted on the fence to show where typhus was or had been. In the dooryard of one place, where the grass had been dug up to make one huge grave for many people, a wrinkled, limping woman stood surrounded by nine children, all under fifteen. Two were almost unable to stand, dead-white and shaking from some fever; three others, one only a baby, were covered with huge running sores and scabs. The woman pointed to the grave-mound.

'I have lost every one but these – there are my husband and my sister and my father, and my brother-in-law and his wife. And we have nothing fit to feed these sick children. The condensed milk that the government sends for the children – the president of the town gives it only to his political constituents, the dishonest Socialist!'

This woman and her children, living in miserable squalor, were all that remained of a powerful *zadrouga*. Two long, one-storey white houses, fronting on the street where it turned at right angles, embraced a sort of patio, carpeted with long grass and wild flowers, and shaded by an ancient oak. The entrance to the houses was from the garden, and there was another house behind, with offices, stables, and the *rackia* distillery, where the family made its own plum brandy. Here lived three generations, the women with their husbands, the men with their wives, and each couple with its children – not to mention cousins, aunts, uncles – more than forty people in all, who shared their land and all their property in common. The buildings were wrecked and burned; of the people, some had died in battle, others had been murdered by the Hungarians, and the typhus had done the rest.

'They did terrible things,' said old Samourovitch as we walked back to the train. 'We are happy that we paid the Austrians for all this by beating them so badly in December.' This extraordinary lack of bitterness we found everywhere in Serbia; the people seemed to think that the smashing Austrian defeat revenged them for all those black enormities, for the murder of their brothers, for the bringing of the typhus.

Through meadows gorgeous with purple larkspur and buttercups, through orchards heavy with peach, apple, cherry, and plum blossoms we went; here the Turkish influence entirely died out, and the mud houses became entirely Serb – capped no longer with red tiles, but with peaked roofs of rough wooden shingles. Then appeared once more over the westward plain the green Bosnian mountains, and we were at Losnitza – again under the Austrian guns across the Drina.

There was a typhus hospital, which we visited. It had once been a school. As the Serbian doctor opened the doors of room after room, a sickening stench of dirt, filthy clothing and airlessness came out. The windows were all closed. The sick – mostly soldiers in the wreck of their uncleaned uniforms – lay packed closely shoulder to shoulder upon foul straw spread on the floor. There was no sign of disinfectant. Some leaned weakly on their elbows, scratching feebly for vermin; others tossed and chattered in delirium, and others lay whitely still, their eyes half open, like the dead.

'It gets better every day,' said the doctor, rubbing his hands. 'Two weeks ago we had four hundred here – now there are only eighty-six ...' He glanced meditatively at the sick men jammed so close together that they almost lay upon one another. 'Then we were *crowded*.'

At dusk we sat at a café table in the great square of Losnitza, drinking Turkish coffee and eating black bread and *kaymak* – delicious yellow cheese-butter. In the dim evening light oxen knelt by their carts, and peasants all in white linen stood in bright groups, talking. From ten different doors of drinking-shops about the immense space, floods of yellow light poured, and there came bursts of violin music and singing. We got up and strolled over to one; the proprietress, a scrawny woman with yellow hair, caught sight of us, and raised a shrill yell: 'Why do you stand there in the street? Why do you not come here and sit at my tables? I have all sorts of good wine, beer, and *koniak!*' We meekly obeyed.

'We are Americans,' I explained as best I could, 'and we do not know your language.'

'That's no reason why you can't drink!' she cried brazenly, and slapped me on the back. 'I don't care what language you drink in!'

Inside two gypsies were playing, one a fiddle and the other a cornet, while an old peasant, his head thrown back, intoned through his nose the ballad of the Bombardment of Belgrade:

THE BOMBARDMENT OF BELGRADE

'A dream had Madame Georgina,
The faithful spouse of Nicola Pachitch
The well-known Serbian prime minister;
In her palace in the centre of Belgrade
She had a dream, and this was her dream:

'Northward the earth trembles –

Trembled Srem, Batchka and Hungary –
And a terrible darkness
Rolls south upon Belgrade,
The White City that rides the waters.
Athwart the gloom lightnings cross,
And thunder follows after,
Smiting the houses and the palaces,
Wrecking the villas and hotels
And the fine shops of Belgrade.
From the Save and the Danube
Soar the roaring water-dragons –
Spitting thunder and lightnings
Over Belgrade, the White City;
Blasting houses and streets,
Reducing to ruin hotels and palaces,
Smashing the wooden pavements,
Burning the pretty shops,
And upsetting churches and chapels;
Everywhere the screams of children and invalids –
Everywhere the cries of old women and old men!
As if the last terrible Day of Judgment
Broke over Belgrade!

'Then in the night Madame Georgina awoke,
Asking herself what had happened,
And began to weep,
For she knew not how to interpret her dream.
Then awoke Nicola Pachitch also
And addressed his faithful spouse:

' "What is the matter with thee, faithful spouse,
That thou risest in the night
And wettest thy cheek with tears?
Of what art thou frightened?
Tell it me, my faithful spouse,
Whom God bless!"

'Then spoke Madame Pachitch:

' "My master! Pachitch, Nicola!
This night have I had a terrible dream.
I have dreamed, and in my dream have seen many things.
But I cannot interpret them,
Therefore am I miserable and worried."

And she began to tell her dream...'

(Three hundred lines more, consisting mostly of accurate prophecy by Mr Pachitch on what actually occurred.)

Over the sharp, crumpled house roofs westward the swollen cupola of a Greek church rose black against the warm yellow sky. And there were great trees, spread like lace across the firmament, where already faint stars glittered. A thin crescent moon floated up over the shadowy Bosnian mountains, the heart and birthplace of Serbian song – dear land so long an exile...

Seven

RUSSIA'S BACK DOOR

At the end of May the Russian army, to the astonishment of the world, had covered more than two hundred miles on its stupendous retreat from the Carpathians. In Bucovina it abandoned Czernowitz before the formidable Austrian drive, and withdrew behind the River Pruth. We decided to cross the frontier where Rumanian Moldavia, Austrian Bucovina, and Russian Bessarabia meet at the bend of the river, and try to strike the Russian front in action.

From Dorohoi, the northern terminus of the Rumanian railway, it is twenty miles over the hills to the frontier. We bargained for a four-horse coach; but the chief of police of Dorohoi smiled and shook his head.

'You cannot pass the frontier without permission from the high authorities,' he said; 'the Rumanian custom-house is closed.' He looked us over thoughtfully. 'However, I am going across to Russia myself tonight, and you can come with me in my automobile if you like. I will introduce you to the commandant of Novo Sielitza, which is the headquarters of the Third Army .... He is a close friend of mine – I often visit him. The Russians are hospitable people. By the way, they will be grateful to you over there if you bring a little something alcoholic –'

Joyously we sallied forth and bought cognac and dismissed our coach. And just as grey evening flooded the world after a day of rain, and the clouds rolled back like curtains, piling up to golden pinnacles in a shallow green sky, our machine roared out from the dripping forest of Hertza, and we could see beyond the white walls and thatched roofs of a little village the rolling miles of hills, emerald with wheat glittering wetly, black with forests, smoking with the sweat of fat earth after rain; and farther still, to the left, the rolling green and gold and brown country of Bucovina – to the right, the plain beyond the Pruth, low hills and higher hills behind – Russian Bessarabia. On the Austrian side, far away, were visible white winding roads, dazzling villas set in green, an occasional shining town – order and prosperity; on the Russian side, the wet tin roofs of a clump of wooden shacks, thatched huts the colour of dirt, a wandering muddy track which served as a road – the very reverse. In all the vast landscape nothing moved, except a mysterious black smoke slowly rising from behind a hill, which is Czernowitz, and steam from a whistling train at Novo Sielitza. But the air trembled with deep, lazy sound – the cannon firing somewhere beyond vision along the Pruth.

Just ahead the river itself came in view between hills, here and there, shining dully like old brass. We swooped down with screaming siren through the village of Hertza, where the peasants, clad in white linen all embroidered with flowers, were gathered on the green for their evening songs and dances and lifted their broad-brimmed hats to us – down, through vineyards and corn-fields, to Mamornitza on the bank of the muddy river.

Over all the west the sunset made a fierce flame, edging the toppling clouds with fire, pouring green gold over the fields. The radiance faded; by the time we reached the riverside it was quite dark, except for a broad red band low down in the northern sky. Against this reared a tumble-down shed set in a barren waste of sand, stones, and mud – where the Pruth roared in the spring floods. But it was Russia, Holy Russia – sombre, magnificent, immense, incoherent, unknown even to herself.

They had been notified at the deserted custom-house, and in a room musty with long neglect a shabby little man viséed our passports. Escorted by two soldiers, we picked our way down to the river, where a flat-bottomed scow lay half full of water, and a rope fastened to the bank stretched out into the darkness – to Russia! We couldn't see the other side, but as we swung out into the brown current, the Rumanian shore glided astern and disappeared; for a moment we were adrift on a boundless sea, and then against the dim, red sky something rose and loomed – a giant soldier with a long-bayoneted rifle, the crown of his hat peaked up in front as only Russians wear it. Beside him was the shadowy form of a two-horse carriage.

Without a word the sentry put our baggage into the carriage and we followed. He leaped to the box – we were off through deep sand, whip cracking .... A sudden guttural hail from the dark, and another huge soldier bulked in the night beside the carriage. Our sentry handed him a slip of paper, which he pretended to read, holding it upside down – although it was now quite dark and he quite illiterate.

'*Koracho!* Good!' he grunted and waved us on. '*Pajal'st!*'

The last red light had faded from the sky, and we rattled through a starless gloom troubled with the confused sounds of an army at rest. Far away on our right accordions jiggled flatly, and a mighty chorus of deep voices swelled in a slow, stern song.

To the left suddenly opened a meadow bright with many fires. Horses were picketed all about – in one corner two stallions strained, screaming, at their ropes. High saddles, sleeping-rugs of rich colour, brass samovars lay on the ground, and on the flames copper pots smoked. In little knots at the fires, flat-faced, swarthy men squatted, Eastern fashion, between their knees – men with Chinese eyes and cheek-bones polished like teak, robed in long caftans and crowned with towering shaggy hats of fur. The twanging, indolent sound of their speech reached us. One stood upright in the firelight, which gleamed on the silver bosses of his belt and the long curved *yataghan* inlaid with gold that hung by his side.

'*Turkmiene,*' explained the soldier on the box.

Turcomans from beyond the Caspian, from the steppes of Asia – the boiling geyser that deluged Europe with the great Mongolian invasions – the mysterious cradle of humankind. The fathers of these warriors followed Ghenghis Khan and Tamerlane and Attila. Their cousins were Sultans in Constantinople, and sat upon the Dragon Throne in Peking. One glimpse we had of them, a tiny handful in the mighty hordes that Russia is pouring down on the West – and then we were among the ruins of Austrian Novo Sielitza, the old frontier.

Here the gaping windows of roofless houses, walls charred and toppling, immense customs warehouses crumpled with fire. The Russians had wrecked everything at the beginning of the war – what became of the people we didn't like to think. A big stucco hotel had been struck by a bursting shell; light shone from within, and big-booted soldiers in blouses stood silhouetted in the doorways. The road we drove on was white and smooth. Shadowy horsemen jingled past, stray light catching the guardless hilts of Cossack swords. Gleaming white linen in the gloom marked Moldavian peasants shuffling along, laughing and speaking gently their Italianate dialect.

A bridge with another sentry, who waved us by when he saw the flash of white paper – now we were in Russian Novo Sielitza. Here there was no destruction; but instead of a hard road, we rocked through a wide expanse of muddy pools and dried ruts, scored with a thousand tracks. At each side of this street was a deep ditch for drainage and sewage, spanned by wooden foot-bridges. Wide, sprawling wooden houses alternated with blocks of tiny Jewish shops, swarming with squealing, whining, bargaining people, and emitting that stale stench that we know on New York's lower East Side. Old Jews in long overcoats, derby hats resting on their ears, scraggly beards, elbows and hands gesticulating – the comedy Jew in a burlesque show – filthy babies crawling in the lamplight, rows of women in Mother Hubbards and brown wigs, nursing their babies and gossiping shrill Yiddish on the door-step.

We swung into a side street, black as pitch, lined on either side by long wooden houses behind picket fences.

'Here we are,' said our guide. 'Now you will see a real Russian house and family.'

The door popped open and a stout, bearded officer stood on the threshold holding a lamp over his head – Captain Vladimir Constantinovitch Madji, commandant of Novo Sielitza. Behind was a bristling bald-headed man with fierce white mustache and goatee, and over his shoulder appeared a grinning face like the face of a very fat little boy, smoking a cigarette, a white silk kerchief wound tightly around his forehead.

'Please! Please! *Povtim!*' said the captain in Rumanian, making gestures of welcome. '*Pajal'st!*' cried the others in Russian.

The chief of police explained that he had brought two friends, *Amerikanska*; they burst forth into another delighted chorus of '*Povtim! Pajal'st!*' and pushed out to look at us, talking rapid Russian.

'They speak neither Russian nor Rumanian. Only French –'

'*Entrez!*' said the captain, with an elementary accent; then in just as amateurish German: '*Kommen Sie herein, meine Herren!*'

'*Voilà! Comment! Comment! Voilà!*' the bald-headed man roared.

'It is all my brother knows of French!' explained Madji, as

we entered. The fat face turned out to belong to a girl of astonishing corpulence and terrific exuberance. Puffing furiously at her cigarette, she squeezed both our hands, grasped the lapels of our coats and shook us, shouting Russian remarks, and laughing uproariously when we didn't understand.

The captain radiated hospitality. 'Alexandra Alexandrovna, get the samovar!'

She ran off, bellowing orders to invisible servants. 'Antonina Feodorovna! *Prinissitié samovarou!*' And in a moment she was back with a new yellow kerchief around her head, a new cigarette, puffing clouds of smoke.

Madji indicated her with his hand. '*Mon mari!* My husband!' he said in his bad French.

His brother pranced up like a little old stallion, also pointing to her; he repeated 'My husband!' adding in a fierce voice: '*Très jolie! Très jolie! Très jolie!*' He said '*très jolie*' over and over again, delighted at remembering another French phrase....

As to the fat girl, we never did discover whose 'husband' she was .... And there was also Alexandra Antonovna, a solemn little girl of about thirteen with the sophisticated eyes of a grown woman, like all Russian little girls; her status in the household remained a mystery, too. Anyway, it wasn't of the least importance, for this was Russia, where such things don't matter....

In the dining-room we began by drinking glass after glass of tea. Boxes of cigarettes overflowed on the table. At one end sat Alexandra Alexandrovna, lighting one cigarette from another, shaking with laughter and shouting at anybody and everybody. At the other end was the old man, beaming upon us and crying: '*Voilà! Comment! Très jolie!*' Antonina the servant shuffled in and out, taking part in the general conversation, arguing every order, bringing fresh water for the samovar – on terms of perfect equality.

Robinson explained to the old man that he looked exactly like Gogol's Cossack hero, Taras Bulba. He was delighted. And from that time on we never addressed him except as 'General Taras Bulba.'

From time to time other officers dropped in – men in belted Russian blouses buttoned up the neck, their hair cropped close. They kissed Alexandra's hand, and made the rounds of the table, murmuring their names. Most of them spoke some French or German, and all were astonishingly frank about the situation.

'Yes, we are falling back like the devil. It is mostly because we lack munitions; but there are other things. Graft – disorganization –'

A lieutenant broke in: 'Do you know the story about Colonel B – ? He had a bad record in the Japanese War, but when this one broke out he was appointed chief of staff to General Ivanov. It was he who forced the beginning of the retreat from the Carpathians; when Ivanov was absent he ordered the retreat of an entire army corps – exposing the flank of the next army. There wasn't any reason for it. People say he is insane .... However, the thing was hushed up, and he became chief of staff to General Dimitriev and did the same thing over again! You'd think that would finish him? Ah, no! He had powerful friends in Petrograd – and now he is chief of staff to another general!'

Said another calmly: 'It is like that. Advance, retreat. Advance, retreat. If we retreat now – why, then, we shall advance again.'

'But how long will the war last?'

'What do we care how long it lasts?' remarked a second captain with a grin: 'What do we care – so long as England gives money and the earth gives men?'

At about ten o'clock Alexandra suddenly decided to dine. She and Antonina set the table, while Taras Bulba bustled about, giving contradictory orders. For *zakouska* there were plates of sardines, smoked and raw herrings, tunny, caviar, sausage, shirred eggs, and pickles – to sharpen the appetite – washed down with seven different kinds of liquor: cognac, benedictine, kümmel, raspberry and plum brandies, and Kiev and Bessarabian wines. Afterward came great platters of corn-meal *polenta*, then chunks of pork and potatoes. We were twelve. The company began dinner with wine-glasses full of cognac followed by the others in rotation, and finished with several cups of Turkish coffee and the seven different liquors all over again. Then the samovar was brought, and we settled down to the eternal *chai*. It was midnight.

'Ah,' cried an officer, 'if we only had vodka now!'

'Is it really forbidden in Russia?'

'Except in the first-class restaurants of the big cities – Kiev, Odessa, Moscow. You can also get foreign drinks. But they are very expensive .... You see, the object of the *ukase* was to keep alcohol from the lower classes; the rich can still get it....'

A young fellow named Amethystov, lieutenant in a Crimean Tartar regiment, asked us if we had heard the story of the Bismarck *Denkmal*.

'It was during the retreat from East Prussia, after Tannenberg,' he said, a gentle smile lighting his blank, fanatical face, 'and my regiment was at Johannisberg, where there was a bronze statue of Bismarck about twelve feet tall – like hundreds all over Germany. My Tartars wanted to pull it down and take it with them as a trophy, but the general absolutely refused to allow it. "It would cause an international incident," said he. As if the war weren't enough of an international incident! Well, so we stole it – pulled it down at night, stood it upright in a field furnace, and covered it over with a tarpaulin. But we couldn't hide the great bronze feet sticking out at the bottom .... We got it as far as Tilsit – and one day the general came riding along the line, and saw the feet!

' "Who took that thing?" he shouts. Oh, how mad he was! "In the morning I'll find out the guilty ones, if I have to court-martial the entire regiment! It must be abandoned here – do you understand me?"

'Of course, he had a right to be angry, because we were using four army horses to pull the thing, and we'd had to abandon a lot of baggage because transport was lacking....

'So that night we took Bismarck out of his cart and set him up in a field, and had a farewell celebration around him .... I remember we made speeches and broke champagne bottles on him. And next day, lo and behold, he was gone – stolen by a Siberian infantry regiment .... Who knows where he is now?' he mused. 'Perhaps retreating across Galicia with the Siberians.'

At the other end of the table a captain of Atamanski Cossacks, his narrow eyes glowing, was saying: 'You have seen the hiltless Cossack sword?' He showed us his own. 'It is terrible in their hands! They slash with a sidelong stroke – whiz! It cuts a man in half! Beautiful! But they love to kill. When prisoners surrender to them, they say always to their colonel: "*Aga!* Let us cut them! It will disgrace us to bring back babies as prisoners!" '

We tried to explain our purpose in coming, but the captain always interrupted with an expansive smile:

'You shall go where you please, my friends. Tomorrow we will arrange all that .... Now eat and drink, eat and drink –'

Alexandra Alexandrovna screamed pleasantries from a cloud of smoke:

'It's not polite when you come to visit friends, to talk of going away!'

'*Très jolie!*' bellowed Taras Bulba. 'You shall not leave here until you have taught me to speak French, German, Spanish, Italian and Chinese! I have a passion for languages –'

It was now one o'clock in the morning; we were worn out. '*Voyons!*' expostulated Madji. 'To sleep is a ridiculous way to pass the night ....'

Eight

BREAKING INTO BUCOVINA

Early the next morning we came out of our lodgings to the shrill sound of Yiddish blessings and reproaches mixed, and found the Jew smirking and rubbing his hands.

'What's the carriage?' I asked, suspecting further extortion. The Jew pointed to a temporary scaffolding such as is used for digging artesian wells, upon which sat an incredibly discouraged-looking *mujik*. On closer inspection we discovered wheels, fastened to arbitrary places with bits of wire and rope; and apparently unattached to the structure, two aged and disillusioned horses leaned against each other.

'B-r-r-r-r-r!' said the *mujik* to these animals, implying that they would run away if he didn't. 'B-r-r-r-r!'

We mounted, while the Jew abusively impressed upon his driver that we were to be taken to Zalezchik, through Boyan and Zastevna; he also told him to get whatever money he could out of us.... At the end of this tirade, the peasant rose and stolidly beat the horses with a long string fastened to a stick, shouting hoarsely: 'Ugh! Eagh! Augh!' The horses awoke, sighed, and moved experimentally – by some mechanical miracle the wheels turned, a shudder ran along our keel, and we were off!

Across the bridge into Austrian Novo Sielitza we rattled, and out upon the hard road that led frontward, slowly gaining upon and passing a long train of ox-carts driven by soldiers and loaded with cases of ammunition. Now we were in Bucovina. On the left, low fields green with young crops stretched flatly to the trees along the Pruth, beyond which rose the rich hills of Rumania; to the right the valley extended miles to cultivated rolling country. Already the June sun poured down windless, moist heat. The driver slumped gradually into his spine, the horses' pace diminished to a merely arithmetical progression, and we crawled in a baking pall of dust like Zeus hidden in his cloud.

'Hey!' We beat upon his back. 'Shake a leg, Dave!'

He turned upon us a dirty, snub-nosed face, and eyes peering through matted hair, and his mouth cracked slowly in an appalling, familiar grin – with the intelligent expression of a loaf of bread. We christened him immediately Ivan the Horrible....

'Ooch!' he cried with simulated ferocity, waving the string. 'Aich! Augh!'

The horses pretended to be impressed, and broke into a shuffle; but ten minutes later Ivan was again rapt in contemplation of the infinite, the horses almost stationary, and we moved in white dust....

Slowly we drew near the leisurely sound of the cannon, that defined itself sharply out of the all-echoing thunder audible at Novo Sielitza. And topping a steep hill crowned with a straggling thatched village, we came in sight of the batteries. They lay on the hither side of an immense rolling hill, where a red gash in the fields dribbled along for miles. At intervals of half a minute a gun spat heavily; but you could see neither smoke nor flame – only minute figures running about, stiffening, and again springing to life. A twanging drone as the shell soared – and then on the leafy hills across the river puffs of smoke unfolding. Over there were the towers of white Czernowitz, dazzling in the sun. The village through which we passed was populous with great brown soldiers, who eyed us sullenly and suspiciously. Over a gateway hung a Red Cross flag, and along the road trickled a thin, steady stream of wounded – some leaning on their comrades, others bandaged around the head, or with their arms in slings; and peasant carts jolted by with faintly groaning heaps of arms and legs. . . .

The road slanted down until we were close to the crashing batteries. For hours we drove along behind a desultory but gigantic artillery battle. Gun after gun after gun, each in its raw pit, covered with brush to shield it from aeroplanes. Sweating men staggered under the weight of shells, moving about the shining caissons; methodically the breech snapped home and the pointer singsonged his range; a firer jerked the lanyard – furious haze belched out, gun recoiled, shell screamed – miles and miles of great cannon in lordly syncopation.

In the very field of the artillery peasants were calmly ploughing with oxen, and in front of the roaring guns a boy in white linen drove cattle over the hill toward the pastures along the river. We met long-haired farmers, with orange poppies in their hats, unconcernedly driving to town. Eastward the world rolled up in another slow hill that bore curved fields of young wheat, running in great waves before the wind. Its crest was torn and scarred with mighty excavations, where multitudinous tiny men swarmed over new trenches and barbed-wire tangles. This was the second-line position preparing for a retreat that was sure to come. . . .

We swung northward, away from the artillery, over the bald shoulder of a powerful hill. Here the earth mounted in magnificent waves, patterned with narrow green, brown, and yellow fields that shimmered under the wind. Through valleys whose sides fell like a bird's swoop were vistas of chequered slopes and copses soft with distance. Far to the west the faint blue crinkly line of the Carpathians marched across the horizon. Tree-smothered villages huddled in the immense folds of the land – villages of clay houses unevenly and beautifully moulded by hand, painted spotless white with a bright blue stripe around the bottom, and elaborately thatched.

Many were deserted, smashed, and black with fire – especially those where Jews had lived. They bore marks of wanton pillage – for there had been no battle here – doors beaten in, windows torn out, and lying all about the wreckage of mean furniture, rent clothing. Since the beginning of the war the Austrians had not come here. It was Russian work....

Peasants smiling their soft, friendly smile took off their hats as we went by. A gaunt man with a thin baby in his arms ran forward and kissed my hand when I gave him a piece of chocolate. Along the roadside stood hoary stone crosses inscribed with sacred verses in the old Slavonic, before which the peasants uncovered and crossed themselves devoutly. And there were rude wooden crosses, as in Mexico, to mark the spots where men had been assassinated....

In a high meadow overlooking the distant river and the far-rolling plains of Bucovina we came upon a camp of Turcomans – their saddled horses staked to graze and their fires burning. Cruel-faced and slant-eyed, they squatted about the cook-pots or moved among the horses, barbaric notes of colour in this green northern field, where, perhaps, their ancestors had camped with Attila a thousand years ago. Beyond the river cousins of theirs lay in the enemy's trenches – beyond the ethereal mountains in the west was Hungary, the rich land where the scourges of God from Asia had finally come to rest. Where the road dipped again into the valley was an old stone chapel, circular in form and surrounded by a graceful colonnade. It was now gutted, and the horses of Turcoman officers were stabled inside....

At any cross-roads we always knew the right road to take, because Ivan invariably took the other. Although born and bred at Novo Sielitza, fifteen miles away, he had never travelled so far abroad. Worse, his porous memory could no longer hold the name of our destination, no matter how often he repeated it. Every little while he turned and peered at us, groaning. 'Zalezchik!' we shouted in chorus, and he fell to

larruping the horses with uncouth cries. He pulled up sometimes, until we pointed to a native and made signs for him to
ask the way.

'Good day,' mumbled Ivan. 'Which is the road to –'

'The road to where, friend?' asked the man.

Ivan scratched his head.

'Where do you want to go?'

Ivan grinned sheepishly.

'Zalezchik!' we bawled – and Ivan repeated – 'Ah, yes,
Zalezchik!'

At noon, we zigzagged up a steep mountain into a pine
forest, and met a long train of trucks coming down, loaded
with the steel floats of a pontoon bridge. Big Don Cossacks
on wiry ponies escorted it, their hair-tufts sticking rakishly
out under their caps.

'*Aie, Barin!*' shouted one of the drivers, pointing southwest.
'*Eto* Pruth? Is that the Pruth?'

I nodded.

'Two days!' he cried, patting his pontoon. 'Two days we
cross the river. . . . Czernowitz!'

Still they passed, clanging along the top of the mountain. We
plunged down through the forest, meeting the great wagons
crawling up with shouts and snapping whips. Steeper and
steeper; the trees thinned, and suddenly fell away altogether,
and the tremendous panorama of the valley of the Dniester
opened out – squares and parallelograms and arcs of vari-
egated colour clashing and weaving in a mighty tapestry of
fertile fields, great rounded folds of earth, sweeping grandly
like the ground swell, rambling white granges ship-like along
the ribbony roads, and villages lost in the hollows. The pon-
toon-trucks staggered up, drawn each by eight horses and
twenty soldiers who pushed, shouting in unison – for a mile
down the hill the road was filled with lumbering big floats
rocking from side to side, straining horses flecked with white

foam, broad-shouldered men curbed with an agony of effort....

Now we were entering a new land. Though the peasants still wore white linen, their head-dress changed; some wore tall round caps of black fur, others high, bell-crowned hats such as Welsh women used to wear. The Slavonic crosses gave way to tall Catholic crucifixes, decked with all the instruments of the Passion – the spear, the sponge, the gloves, the hammer. We met people who spoke no Rumanian – Polish began to replace it. Granges where whole patriarchal families had lived stood along the road – immense houses containing living-rooms, stables, barns all under one roof, with a road running through the middle of the building from front to back. It was a blasted country, seared with battle, and with the triple passing of two great armies. The trampled grain was sickly yellow in the fields; whole villages in ruins gaped empty, except for Russian soldiers, and few men were to be seen except the aged and crippled – only women and children, with furtive eyes and sunken faces. In the fields among the growing crops old trenches crumbled in, and rusty barbed-wire entanglements straggled through the wheat everywhere. For miles along the left side of the road gigantic new trenches and artillery positions were building in frantic haste. Thousands of soldiers swarmed over the landscape, the afternoon sun flashing on their lifted spades. Wagons loaded with tools and barbed wire impeded the road. Near Zastevna, we saw peasant women and children digging under the super-intendence of non-commissioned officers, a long file of them carrying out the dirt in head baskets. Why this feverish activity here, twenty miles behind the positions occupied by the Russians only a month before?

Nine

ZALEZCHIK THE TERRIBLE

It was on the other side of Zastevna, where we stopped beside some ruined houses for a drink, that we saw the Austrian prisoners. They came limping along the road in the hot sun, about thirty of them, escorted by two Don Cossacks on horseback; grey uniforms white with dust, bristly faces drawn with fatigue. One man had the upper left-hand part of his face bound up, and the blood had soaked through; another's hand was bandaged, and some jerked along on improvised crutches. At a sign from the Cossacks, who dismounted, they reeled and stumbled to the side of the road, and sullenly threw themselves down in the shade. Two dark-faced men snarled at each other like beasts. The man with the wounded head groaned. He with the bandaged hand began tremblingly to unwrap the gauze. The Cossacks goodnaturedly waved us permission to talk with them, and we went over with handfuls of cigarettes. They snatched at them with the avidity of smokers long deprived of tobacco – all except one haughty-faced youth, who produced a handsome case crammed with gold-tipped cigarettes, declined ours frigidly, and took one of his own, without offering any to the others.

'He is a Count,' explained a simple, peasant-faced boy with awe.

The man with the wounded hand had got his bandage off at last, and was staring at his bloody palm with a sort of fascination.

70

'I think this had better be dressed again,' said he at last, glancing diffidently at a stout, sulky-looking person who wore a Red Cross arm-band. The latter looked across with lazy contempt and shrugged his shoulders.

'We've got some bandages,' I began, producing one. But one of the Cossacks came over, scowling and shaking his head at me. He kicked the Red Cross man with a look of disgust, and pointed to the other. Muttering something, the stout man fumbled angrily in his case, jerked out a bandage, and slouched across.

There were thirty of them, and among that thirty-five races were represented: Tcheks, Croats, Magyars, Poles and Austrians. One Croat, two Magyars, three Tcheks could speak absolutely not a word of any language but their own, and, of course, none of the Austrians knew a single word of Bohemian, Croatian, Hungarian, or Polish. Among the Austrians were Tyroleans, Viennese, and a half-Italian from Pola. The Croats hated the Magyars, and the Magyars hated the Austrians – and as for the Tcheks, no one would speak to them. Besides, they were all divided up into sharply defined social grades, each of which snubbed its inferiors.... As a sample of Franz Joseph's army the group was most illuminating.

They had been taken in a night attack along the Pruth, and marched more than twenty miles in two days. But they were all enthusiastic in praise of their Cossack guards.

'They are very considerate and kind,' said one man. 'When we stop for the night the Cossacks personally go around to each man, and see that he is comfortable. And they let us rest often....

'The Cossacks are fine soldiers,' another broke in; 'I have fought with them, and they are very brave. I wish we had cavalry like them!'

A young volunteer of the Polish legion asked eagerly if Rumania was coming in. We replied that it seemed like it, and suddenly he burst out, quivering:

'My God! My God! What can we do? How long can this awful war last? All we want is peace and quiet and rest! We are beaten – we are honourably beaten. England, France, Russia, Italy, the whole world is against us. We can lay down our arms with honour now! Why should this useless butchery go on?'

And the rest sat there, gloomily listening to him without a word....

Toward evening we were rattling down a steep gully between high cliffs. A stream plunged down beside the road, turning a hundred water-wheels whose mills lay shattered by artillery fire; shacks in partial ruin shouldered each other along the gully, and on top of the eastern cliff we could see disembowelled trenches and an inferno of twisted, snarled barbed wire, where the Russians had bombarded and stormed the Austrian defences a month before. Hundreds of men were at work up there clearing away the wreckage and building new works. We rounded a corner suddenly and came out upon the bank of the Dniester, just below where the tall railroad bridge plunged into the water its tangle of dynamited girders and cables. Here the river made a huge bend, beneath earthen cliffs a hundred feet high, and across a pontoon bridge choked with artillery the once lovely town of Zalezchik lay bowered in trees. As we crossed, naked Cossacks were swimming their horses in the current, shouting and splashing, their powerful white bodies drenched with golden light....

Zalezchik had been captured, burned, and looted three times by two armies, shelled for fifteen days, and the major portion of its population wiped out by both sides because it had given aid and comfort to the enemy. Night was falling when we drove into the market-place, surrounded with the shocking debris of tall houses. A sort of feeble market was going on there under miserable tilted shacks, where sad-eyed peasant women spread their scanty vegetables and loaves of bread, the centre of a mob of soldiers. A few Jews slunk about the corners. Ivan demanded a hotel, but the man smiled and pointed to a tall crumbling brick wall with 'Grand Hotel' painted boldly across it – all that remained. Where could we get something to eat?

'Something to eat? There is not enough food in this town to feed my wife and children.'

An atmosphere of terror hung over the place – we could feel it in the air. It was in the crouching figures of the Jews, stealing furtively along the tottering walls; in the peasants as they got out of the way of our carriage, doffing their hats; in the faces of cringing children, as soldiers went by. It got dark, and we sat in the carriage, debating what to do.

We bestowed upon Ivan a two-rouble piece, which, after biting, he put away in his pocket with hoarse sounds betokening gratitude. And we left him sitting on his vehicle in the middle of the square, gazing at nothing.

An 'Apteka' – apothecary shop – stood on the corner, comparatively undamaged, with a light inside. I found the druggist alone, a Jew who spoke German.

'What are you?' he asked suspiciously, peering at me.

'An American.'

'There is no hotel here,' he burst out suddenly. 'There is no place to stay and nothing to eat. A month ago the Russians came in here – they slaughtered the Jews, and drove the women and children out there.' He pointed west. 'There is no place here –'

'Then,' I said, 'the military commandant must take care of us. Where can I find him?'

'I will send my assistant with you,' he answered. His face stiffened with fear. 'You will not say to them what I have told, noble *Herr*? You will not –'

The entry of two Russian soldiers interrupted him, and he rose, addressing me insolently for their benefit:

'I can't drive you out of the shop. It's a public shop. But

73

remember, I assume no responsibility for you. I didn't ask you to come here. I don't know you.' For, after all, we might be undesirable people.

When we came out of the Apteka Ivan was still there, hunched over in the same position, and an hour later, when we issued from the colonel's headquarters, he had not moved, though it was quite dark. What was passing in that swampy mind? Perhaps he was trying to remember the name of Novo Sielitza, his home – perhaps he was merely wondering how to get there....

We sat long over dinner with the genial colonel and his staff, chattering politics and gossip in intensely fragmentary German. Among other officers were a young Finnish lieutenant and an old Cossack major with a wrinkled Mongolian face like the pictures of Li Hung Chang, who were very much excited over the sinking of the *Lusitania*, and sure that America would go to war.

'What can we do for you?' asked the colonel.

We said that we would like to visit this part of the front, if there were any fighting going on.

'That, I am afraid, is impossible from here,' he regretted. 'But if you will go to Tarnopol, the general commanding this army will surely give you permission. Then you must return here, and I shall be glad to accompany you myself. A train for Tarnopol leaves to-night at eleven.'

Could he give us any idea what was happening along the front?

'With pleasure,' said he eagerly, telling an orderly to bring the maps. He spread them out on the table. 'Now here, near Zadagora, we have ten big guns placed in these positions, to stop the Austrian flanking column that is rolling up from the Pruth. Over here, near Kalusz, the Austrians imagine that we have nothing but cavalry, but in about three days we'll throw three regiments across this little stream at this point –'

I remarked that all those maps seemed to be German or Austrian maps.

'Oh, yes,' he replied. 'At the beginning of the war we had no maps at all of Bucovina or Galicia. We didn't even know the lay of the land until we had captured some....'

Ten

BEHIND THE RUSSIAN
RETREAT

In the morning we woke stiff and cramped from the benches of our third-class car, and looked out the window upon the boundless Galician steppe, heavy with golden wheat and with ploughed land deeper than velvet; ten-mile planes of flat earth uptilted gently against horizons where giant windmills rode hull down, like ships at sea. We had made thirty miles in nine hours.

The train whistled triumphantly down long inclines, and panted up slopes where the mounting track was visible for miles and miles. Our car was full of officers making the cheerful hubbub that Russians always make together. And from the ten freight-cars full of troops behind came nasal accordion music, the slow roar of big voices singing, shouts and cheers. At little stations where the flat-faced, sombrely dressed Polish peasants and their bright-kerchiefed, broad-hipped women stared stolidly at the train, hundreds of soldiers and officers with teapots jostled each other democratically around the *kipiatok* – the huge tank of boiling water you find at every Russian railway-station – and there was incessant tea. An officer of high rank, who had an orderly, set up a small brass samovar in the next compartment to ours....

From a strap over his shoulder hung a gold-hilted Cossack sword, the gift of the Tsar for bravery – it bore also the tassel of the Order of Vladimir. The orderly, probably a *mujik* from one of his estates, called him familiarly 'Ivan Ivanovitch.'

Presently he came over with true Russian hospitality, and invited us in French to drink a glass of *chai*. We got to talking about the war.

'Nevertheless, it is impossible to beat Russia,' said he.

I objected that Russia had been beaten many times.

'You mean the Japanese War. I served in Manchuria myself, and I think I can tell you why we were beaten. In the first place the peasants knew nothing of the causes of the war, and no one took the trouble to tell them. They had never heard of the Japanese. "We are not angry with the Japanese, whoever they may be," said the *mujiks*. "Why should we fight them?"

'And then everything was horribly mismanaged. I have seen troops, worn out and half starved by a forty days' railway journey on insufficient food, detrained and sent into battle without an hour's rest. And there was the vodka, too, which we haven't got to reckon with to-day. Before the battle of Mukden I saw whole regiments lying in a drunken sleep on the ground.... It was an unpopular war – there was no patriotism among the peasants.'

'And is there patriotism now?'

'Yes, they are very patriotic – they hate the Germans. You see, most of the agricultural machinery comes from Germany, and this machinery does the work of many men, driving the peasants into the factories at Petrograd and Moscow and Riga and Odessa. Then the Germans flood Russia with cheap goods which undersell Russian products – which causes our factories to shut down and throws thousands out of work. In the Baltic provinces, too, German landlords own all the soil, and the peasants live miserably.... Wherever in Russia they have no feeling against the Germans, we tell them these things.... Oh, yes, this time the Russians know why they are fighting!'

'So the peasants think that by beating the Germans they will get rid of poverty and oppression?'

He nodded good-humoredly. Robinson and I both had the same thought: if the peasants were going to beat any one, why didn't they begin at home? Afterward we discovered that they *were* beginning at home.

Late in the morning we stopped within sight of the towers of Tarnopol, alongside a huge hospital-train which was marked with the imperial arms and bore the legend: 'Sanitary Train, Gift of the Imperatrice Alexandra Feodorovna.'

'Come on,' said our friend, ordering his baggage out. 'We had better change trains. Ours will probably stay here until afternoon.'

We swung aboard the hospital-train just as it left, and found ourselves in a little car divided into two compartments by a rough board partition. Wooden bunks were folded up against the sides; in one corner was a stove covered with dirty pots and pans; trunks, a tin wash-basin on a box fastened to the wall, and clothes suspended from nails, gave it the look of a ship's forecastle.

In one compartment sat two middle-aged minor officers, and in the other a stout, comfortable-looking woman and a young girl. The two men and the women were smoking cigarettes, and throwing the butts on the maculate floor; steaming glasses of tea littered the tables; the windows were closed.

The girl spoke German and a little French; the woman was her mother, the grizzled sanitary lieutenant her father, and the second captain of engineers her uncle. Since the beginning of the war ten months ago they had been living in this car, travelling from Vilna and Kiev to the front, and back again with the wounded.

'My mother wouldn't let my father go to the war without her, and she made so much fuss that he took us both.... And my uncle's father-in-law is a Collegiate Assessor and a Judge in the government of Minsk, so he managed to get us this car to live in.'

'Have you seen any fighting?'

'Twice,' she answered. 'Near Warsaw last winter a German

shell struck one of our cars and blew it to pieces – there we were under artillery fire all day. And only last week, beyond Kalusz, the whole train was captured by Austrians. But they let us go again.... We're bound for Vilna now with a load of wounded. In two days we'll be back there....'

Tea and cigarettes were forthcoming, with the customary large-hearted Russian hospitality, and we sat around while they told us of the pleasures of a perpetual travelling vacation – for all the world like their ancestors, the nomadic Russian tribes.

Tarnopol station was a place of vast confusion. From a long military train poured running soldiers with tin teapots to the *kipiatok*, hurtling a column of infantry that was marching across to another train. Officers shouted and cursed, beating with the flat of their swords. Engines whistled hysterically, bugles blared – calling the men back to their cars. Some hesitated and stopped, undecided whether to go forward or back; others ran faster. Around the hot-water tanks was a boiling, yelling mob. Clouds of steam rose from the pouring faucets.... Hundreds of peasant refugees – Poles, Moldavians, and Hungarians – squatted along the platform waiting stolid and bewildered among their bundles and rolls of bedding; for as they retreated the Russians were clearing the country of every living thing and destroying houses and crops.... The station-master waved futile hands in the centre of a bawling crowd of officers and civilians, all flourishing passes and demanding when their various trains departed....

An armed sentry at the door tried to stop us, but we pushed by. He made a half-motion with his rifle, took a step and paused irresolutely, bellowing something about passes – and we went on. A hundred spies could have entered Tarnopol....

'*Na Stap!*' we cried to the cabby: 'To the Staff! Along the railroad yards on each side were mountains of sacks and boxes higher than the houses. Tarnopol was a city of solid

Polish architecture, with occasional big modern German buildings, and sudden vistas of narrow busy streets lined with hundreds of shops, all painted with signs picturing the goods sold within; streets swarming with Jews in long black coats and curly brimmed black hats. Here they looked better off and less servile than in Novo Sielitza. As everywhere in Galicia and Poland, there was a smell of combined 'kosher,' boot-leather, and what we call 'Polak'; it filled the air, tainted the food we ate, and impregnated our very bedclothes.

Half-way down the street we met a column of soldiers marching four abreast toward the railway station, bound for the front. Less than a third had rifles.

They came tramping along with the heavy, rolling pace of booted peasants, heads up, arms swinging – bearded giants of men with dull, brick-red hands and faces, dirty-brown belted blouses, blanket-rolls over their shoulders, intrenching-tools at their belts, and great wooden spoons stuck in their boot-tops. The earth shook under their tread. Row after row of strong, blank, incurious faces set westward toward unknown battles, for reasons incomprehensible to them. And as they marched, they sang – a plain chant and tremendous as a Hebrew psalm. A lieutenant at the head of the column sang one bar, the first sergeant took him up – and then like a damned-up river burst the deep easy voice of three thousand men, flung out from great chests in a rising sudden swell of sound, like organs thundering:

> 'For the last time I walk with you my friends –
> For the last time!
> And to-morrow, early in the morning,
> Will weep my mother and my brethren,
> For I am going away to the war!
> And also will weep my sweetheart,
> Whom I have loved for many, many years....
> She whom I hoped one day to go with to the church....
> I swear that I will love her until I die!'

They passed, and the roaring slow chorus rose and fell

crashing fainter and fainter. Now we rode between interminable hospitals, where haggard, white-draped figures leaned listlessly from the windows, bleached yellow from long confinement. Soldiers crowded the streets – wounded men on crutches, old Landwehr veterans, regulars, and boys who couldn't have been more than seventeen. There were three soldiers to every civilian; though that may have been partly due to the fact that many Jews had been 'expelled' when the Russians entered the town – a dark and bloody mystery that. On each corner stood an armed sentry, scrutinizing the passers-by with the menacing look of a suspicious peasant. As we drove by in our Stetson hats, knickerbockers and puttees – never before seen in that country of universal boots – they stared open-mouthed. You could read on their faces the painfully born doubt about us – but by that time we were blocks away.

'*Stowi!*' growled the guard before Staff headquarters, lowering his bayonet. 'Stop! *Shto takoi?*'

We wanted an officer who could speak French or German.

'Are you *Niemetski?*' he asked, using the old peasant word for Germans – meaning 'dumb,' for the first Germans in Russia couldn't speak the language.

'We are Americans.' Other soldiers gathered to listen.

'*Amerikanska!*' said one man with a cunning smile. 'If you are Americans, tell me what language the Americans speak.'

'They speak *Angliiski*.'

At this they all looked inquiringly at the learned soldier, who nodded. An officer appeared, looked us up and down very severely, and asked us in German who we were and what we were doing. We explained. He scratched his head, shrugged his shoulders, and disappeared. Another, a huge bearded man, bustled out now and tried us with Russian, Polish, and broken French. It was evidently a poser for him, too, for he walked vaguely up and down, pulling at his beard. Finally he despatched several orderlies in different directions, and motioned us to follow him. We entered a large room that had evidently been a theatre, for there was a stage at one end hung with a gaudily painted curtain. About thirty men in undress uniform bent over desks, laboriously writing out by hand the interminable documents of bureaucratic routine. One was cautiously experimenting with a new invention, the typewriter, which evidently none of them had ever seen before, and which caused everybody great amusement.

A young officer came out of an inside room, and began to fire stern questions in rapid French. Who were we? What were we doing here? How did we come? We told our story.

'Through Bucovina and Galicia!' he cried in astonishment. 'But no civilians are permitted to enter Bucovina and Galicia!'

We produced our passes.

'You are correspondents? But don't you know that no correspondents can come to Tarnopol?'

We pointed out that in fact we were there. He seemed at a loss.

'What is your business?' said he uncertainly.

I told him that we wanted to visit the front of the Ninth Army, and to find out about certain American citizens in Galicia – at the request of the American minister in Bucharest. He ran his eye down the list of names.

'Bah! Jews!' he remarked disgustedly. 'Why does your country admit Jews to citizenship? Or, if it does, why doesn't it keep them at home? Where do you want to go – Strij? Kalusz? That is not possible!'

'Ah,' I said, 'then Strij and Kalusz are on the first line now?' He grinned. 'No. The second line – the *German* second line?'

We were astounded by the rapidity of the German advance.

'It is only a question of time,' he went on indifferently. 'They will soon be here.' And suddenly he sprang to attention. 'The general!'

The thirty clerks leaped to their feet with one bound.

'Good day, my children,' said a pleasant voice.

'Good day to your generalship!' shouted the clerks in unison – and sat down again to their work.

General Lichisky was a man under middle age, with a keen, smiling face. He saluted us and cordially shook hands.

'So you wish to go to the front?' he said, when the officer had explained. 'I don't understand how you managed to get here – for correspondents have not been allowed in Tarnopol at all. However, your papers are perfectly satisfactory. But I cannot permit you to visit the first line; the Grand Duke has issued an order absolutely forbidding it. You had better go to Lvov – Lemberg – and see what can be done through Prince Bobrinski, governor-general of Galicia.... I will give you passes. In the meanwhile, you may stay here as long as your business requires it....'

He detailed a young sub-officer who spoke English to look after us, and ordered that we should be lodged at the hotel reserved for officers of the Staff, and dine at the mess.

We wandered about the town. Tarnopol was full of troops – regiments returning from the front for a rest, others going out, still more, fresh troops, arriving from Russia with uniforms yet unsoiled by battle; mighty singing choruses shocked and smashed against each other in a ceaseless surge of big voices. Few of the men had arms. Long wagon-trains loaded with immense quantities of flour, meat, and canned food filed toward the west – but we saw no ammunition.

The young lieutenant told us things. He had been through the Masurian Lakes disaster, and later in the Carpathians.

'Even before the retreat,' he said, 'we didn't have half enough rifles or ammunition. My company, for example, was stationed in two trenches – a front trench and a reserve trench. A third of my men were in the first trench, and they had rifles. All the rest had no rifles – their duty was to go forward, one by one, and pick up the rifles of those who were killed....'

As we walked along, the guards on the corners gathered

and looked at us, whispering, until they made up their minds that we were German spies – then they arrested us and took us to the Prefecture. There no one knew what to do with us, so we were solemnly marched to the Staff, where our friend the French-speaking officer set us free again, loading our captors with abuse. The poor guards slunk away in great bewilderment; their orders were to arrest suspicious-looking persons, and when they did so, they were threatened with the knout. At regular intervals all day we were arrested by new sets of soldiers, and the same farce gone through.

'Beasts!' shouted the officer, shaking his fist at the poor, puzzled soldiers. 'Fools! I'll have you punished!'

We suggested mildly that he might give us a pass which we could show to people when they stopped us, but he said that he had no authority. . . .

Late in the afternoon we stood near the barracks, watching a long column of sullen Austrian prisoners marching in between their guards. A soldier on duty gaped for several minutes at our puttees, let his eyes slowly travel up our costumes, and finally arrested us, and took us up to a major in spectacles who stood on the corner.

He questioned us in German, and I answered. He peered suspiciously over his glasses.

'Where are your passports?'

I said that we had left them at the hotel.

'I think I shall take you to the Staff,' said he.

'We have already been to the Staff,' said I.

'Hum!' he meditated. 'Then to the Police.'

'What is the use of that? We've already been to the Police.'

'Hum!' It was puzzling, so he changed the subject. 'You are correspondents? In what countries have you been?'

'We have just come from Serbia.'

'And how is it in Serbia?'

I said that the sickness was terrible there.

'Sickness!' said he. 'What sickness?' He had never heard of

I HALF-SAVAGE GIANTS DRESSED IN THE ANCIENT PANOPLY OF THAT
CURIOUS SLAVIC PEOPLE WHOSE MAIN BUSINESS IS WAR

2 THE SENTRY,
HOLLOW-CHEEKED, FILTHY, AND STARVED-LOOKING

Graves along the Vardar

An old soldier

Peasant

Soldier

Refugees

3 SERBIA – NISH

4 A HOSPITAL AT NISH. IN THE FEEBLE LIGHT OF TWO LANTERNS
WE COULD SEE THE PATIENTS WRITHING IN THEIR DIRTY BLANKETS

5 DISCHARGED FROM A TYPHUS HOSPITAL

6. AUSTRIAN PRISONERS IN UNIFORM WANDERED FREELY EVERYWHERE WITHOUT A GUARD

7 "A LITTLE AVENGER OF KOSSOVO"

8 MADJI INDICATED HER WITH HIS HAND. "MON MARI!" ["MY HUSBAND!"] HE SAID IN HIS BAD FRENCH.

(BUCOVINA)

9 A SON OF GHENGHIS KHAN, TURCOMAN

10 TURCOMANS FROM BEYOND THE CASPIAN: FROM THE STEPPES OF ASIA

11 BLIND FOR LIFE (KOVEL)

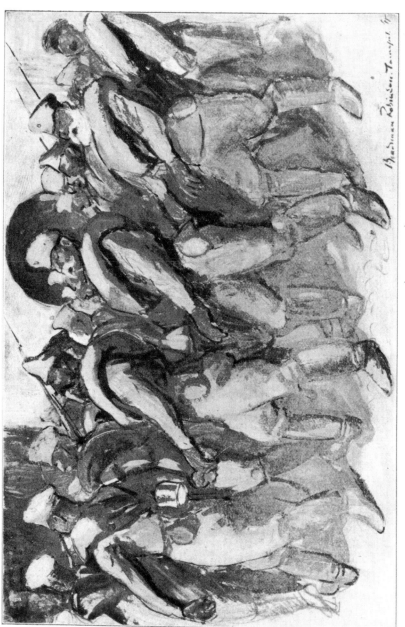

12 CHANTING LEGIONS (LEMBERG)

A pope

The sceptical Colonel Bolatov

Travelling with Austrian prisoners in Bucovina

13 ON THE WAY TO LEMBERG

"They're German spies!"

"But you are not under guard!"

Kubanski Cossack

14 CHOLM

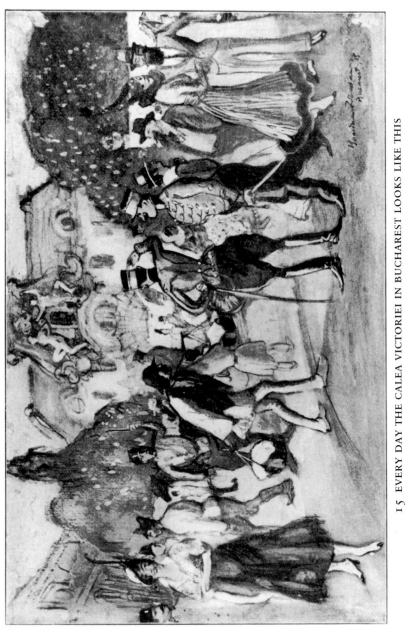

15 EVERY DAY THE CALEA VICTORIEI IN BUCHAREST LOOKS LIKE THIS

16 THE SERB

the typhus. 'Really!' he said indifferently. 'Tell me; will Italy enter the war, do you think?'

'Italy has already been in the war for six weeks.'

'You don't say!' he yawned. 'Well, gentlemen, I must leave you. Very happy to have made your acquaintance – *sehr angenehm....*' and he bowed and walked away.

No one knew when the train for Lemberg left; our officer telephoned to the quartermaster, who called up the chief of transport, who in turn asked the chief of the railway administration. The answer was that everything was so mixed up that there was no certainty – it might leave in five minutes and it might leave to-morrow morning. So we plunged again into the frightful mêlée at the station, stacked our bags against the wall, and sat down to wait. Long files of stretchers bore groaning wounded to hospital-trains, running soldiers jostled each other, officers bawled hoarsely, sweating conductors made despairing gestures about their trains blocked interminably along the tracks. A fat colonel confronted the harassed station-master, pointing to his regiment drawn up along the freight platform as far as the eye could reach.

'Where the devil is my train?' he shouted. The station-master shrugged.

There were cavalry officers in green trousers, with broad sabres; subalterns of the automobile and aeroplane corps who carried blunt, ivory-handled daggers in place of swords; Cossack *atamans* from Ural and Kuban with pointed, turned-up boots, long caftans open in front and laced at the waist, tall fur hats barred on top with gold and red, belts bossed with precious metals and silver-mounted *yataghans*; generals of various degrees of generality. There were club-footed officers, near-sighted officers who couldn't see to read, one-armed and epileptic officers. Minor officials of the postal service and the railway went by dressed like field-marshals and carrying swords. Almost every one wore a uniform with gold or silver shoulder-straps; their number and variety were bewildering. Scarcely an officer whose breast was not decorated with the gold and silver badges of the Polytechnic or the Engineering School, the bright ribbons of the Orders of Vladimir, St George, or St Michael; gold-hilted honour swords were frequent. And every one incessantly saluted every one else. . . .

Seven hours later we boarded the train for Lemberg, and got into a compartment with two shabby, middle-aged lieutenants who were typical of nine-tenths of the minor Russian bureaucrats. We began talking ragged German, and I asked them about the suppression of vodka.

'Vodka!' said one. 'You may be sure they didn't suppress the vodka without making up the money lost in some other way. It is all very well for war-time – you know, the Revolution in 1905 was due entirely to the peasants' getting drunk on vodka – but after the war we shall have vodka again. Everybody wants vodka. They cannot stop it.'

His companion asked if there were compulsory military service in America. I said no.

'Like England,' he nodded. 'That is all very well for you, but in Russia it wouldn't do at all. The peasants wouldn't fight.'

'But I thought the people were very enthusiastic about the war?'

'Pooh!' he answered contemptuously. 'The Russian peasant is a very silly person. He cannot read or write. If you asked him to volunteer, he would say that he was very comfortable where he was, and didn't care to be killed. But when you order him to go, he goes!'

I wanted to know whether there was any organized opposition to the war. The first man nodded.

'Fifteen members of the Duma – they can't execute Duma members – are in prison for sending revolutionary propaganda to the army. The men who circulated it in the ranks have all been shot. They were mostly Jews. . . .'

It took fourteen hours to go forty-five miles. We halted hours on switches to let military trains go by, and long white strings of silent cars that smelled of iodoform. Again miles and miles of wheat-fields yellowing richly – a wonderful harvest here. The country was alive with soldiers. They thronged every station; half-armed regiment slouched along the platform, waiting for their trains; trains of cavalry and their horses, trains of flat cars piled high with supplies, preceded and followed us, or passed going in the other direction. Everywhere utter disorganization – a battalion side-tracked all day without food, and farther on huge dining sheds where thousands of meals were spoiling, because the men didn't come. Engines whistled impatiently for a clear track.... One had an impression of vast forces hurled carelessly here and there, of indifference on a grand scale, of gigantic waste.

How different from the faultless German machine I saw at work in northern France four months after the occupation! There, too, was a problem of transporting millions of men, of hurrying them from one point to another, of carrying arms, ammunition, food, and clothing for them. But although northern France is covered with railroads and Galicia is not, the Germans had built new four-track lines plunging across country and cutting through cities, over bridges made of steel and concrete, erected in eighteen days. In German France trains were never late....

Eleven

LEMBERG BEFORE THE GERMANS CAME

The immense station at Lemberg – or Lvov in Polish – was choked with troops running and calling, with soldiers asleep on the filthy floor, with stupefied refugees wandering vaguely about. No one questioned or stopped us, though Lemberg was one of the forbidden places. We drove through the ancient and royal Polish city, between the gloomy walls of great stone buildings like Roman and Florentine palaces – once the seats of the world's proudest nobility. In little squares among the mediæval twisted streets were Gothic churches of the great period – high, thin roofs, spires of delicate stone tracery, and rich rose-windows. Immense modern German buildings bulked across the noble sky-line, and there were the brilliant shops, restaurants and cafés, wide green squares of a big city. Shabby Jewish quarters encroached on the smart streets, littered with filth and populous with noisy Hebrews, but here their houses and shops were wider, they laughed more, walked more like free people than in the other places we had been. Soldiers – always soldiers – shuffling Jews, and quick, gesticulating Poles – the ugliest race in the world – thronged the sidewalks. Everywhere were wounded men in every stage of convalescence. Whole streets of houses had been turned into temporary hospitals. Never in any country during the war have I seen such vast numbers of wounded as behind the Russian front.

The Hotel Imperial was an old palace. Our room measured

twenty-five feet by thirty, fourteen feet high, and the outside walls were nine feet thick. We breakfasted, lost in the wastes of this vast apartment; and then, because our pass read, 'The bearers must report immediately to the Chancellory of the governor-general of Galicia,' we took our way to the ancient palace of the Polish kings, where the local Russian bureaucracy was functioning with all its clumsy ineffectualness.

A surging crowd of refugees and civilians of all sorts beat about the clerk's desk in the anteroom. Finally he took our pass, read it attentively two or three times, turned it upside down, and handed it back with a shrug of the shoulders. He paid no further attention to us. So we forced our way past several sentries into an inner office, where an officer sat writing at a desk. He looked at the pass and smiled sweetly.

'*Ya nisnayo,*' said he. 'I know nothing about it.'

We asked for some one who could speak French or German, and he went to find one. Three-quarters of an hour later he returned with an oldish captain who spoke some German. We explained that General Lichisky had ordered us to report to the Chancellory, and that we wanted to go the front.

'I will show you. This way.' He mentioned us down a passage. We walked on for some time, and suddenly looking around, missed him. We never saw him again.

Immediately ahead was a door marked 'Staff of the Governor-General,' which we entered, telling the orderly that we wanted to speak to some one who understood French or German. A genial colonel promptly appeared, shaking hands and introducing himself: 'Piotr Stefanovitch Verchovsky, *á votre service.*' We told our tale.

'Please wait a few minutes, gentlemen,' said he, 'and I will arrange your affair.'

He took our pass and disappeared. Four hours later an orderly came into the room and handed me the pass, shrugging his shoulders.

'Where is Colonel Verchovsky?' we demanded.

'*Ne poniemayo!*' he muttered. 'I don't understand!'

I went to the door and sent the orderly to find the colonel; and in a few minutes he appeared, polite as ever, but greatly surprised to see us still there.

'Your pass distinctly says that you must report to the Chancellory,' he explained, 'but I have tried in vain to find the proper department. The truth is that we are in great confusion here on account of this morning's news. I advise you to go to Prince Bobrinski's personal headquarters, and ask to speak with his aide-de-camp, Prince Troubetskoi. . . . But don't say I sent you.'

There were four sets of suspicious sentries to pass on our way to the governor's. We sent in our cards, and were immediately ushered into a room full of smartly dressed officers smoking, laughing and talking, and reading newspapers. One dashing boy in a hussar uniform, surrounded by a gay circle, was telling in French a story about himself and a Polish countess whom he had met at Nice. . . . A gentle-faced, bearded pope of the Russian church, in a long, black-silk soutane, with a huge silver crucifix dangling from a silver neck-chain, paced up and down arm in arm with a bull-necked colonel covered with decorations. . . . Nothing seemed farther from this easy, pleasant-mannered company than war.

A great handsome youth with shining teeth under a heavy mustache came forward, holding out his hand.

'I'm Troubetskoi,' said he in English. 'How on earth did you manage to get here? It is impossible for correspondents to enter Lemberg!'

We produced quantities of passes signed by generals and their chiefs of staff.

'Americans!' he sighed, biting his lips to repress a grin. 'Americans! What's the use of regulations when Americans are about? I don't understand how you found out I was here, or why you came to me.'

We murmured something about having met Troubetskoi the sculptor, in New York.

'Ah yes,' said he. 'That is the international one. He does not speak Russian, I believe.... But now you are here, what can I do for you?'

'We want to go to the front.' Here he shook his head doubtfully. 'At least we thought the governor-general might let us visit Przemysl –'

'I'm sure he would,' grinned the prince, 'but for the regrettable news of this morning. The Austrians entered Przemysl at eight o'clock!'

We had not dreamed that it would fall so soon. 'Do you think they will get to Lemberg?'

'Very probably,' he answered in an uninterested tone. 'Neither are now of any strategic value. We are rectifying our line.' Then changing the subject, he said that he would see the governor-general himself and ask what could be done for us. Would we come in the morning?

The pope, who had been listening, now asked in very good English, what part of America we were from.

'I have been in America for sixteen years,' he said, smiling. 'For eight years I was priest of the Greek church in Yonkers, New York. I came back for the war to help all I could.... Now I only wait for peace to go back yonder.'

As we emerged on the street, a column of gigantic soldiers, four deep, rounded the corner with their tin buckets swinging, tramping to their kitchens for dinner. Just in front of the palace the front rank burst into song, and with a roar the following ranks joined in:

> 'I remember when I was a young girl,
> During the army manœuvres
> To my village came a young officer
> With soldiers, and he said to me,
> 'Give me some water to drink.'
> When he finished drinking, he stooped from his horse
> And kissed me.

Long stood I looking after him as he went away,
And all night I could not sleep –
All night he was in my dreams. . . .
Many years after, when I was a widow
And had married off my four daughters,
To my village came an old general;
And he was broken and wounded with many wounds.
He groaned. When I looked at him my heart beat fast –
It was the same young officer, I could not mistake him:
Brave as ever – the same voice,
Brave as ever – the same eyes,
But many white hairs in his mustache.
And so, as many years ago, this night I cannot sleep,
And all night in my dreams I see him. . . .'

Now through all the streets poured rivers of soldiers singing. We could see their hats flowing along the end of the avenue, over the top of a little rise. Grand choruses met, clashing like cross-seas in the echoing hollows between tall buildings – the city hummed with deep melody. This was the inexhaustible strength of Russia, the powerful blood of her veins spilled carelessly from her bottomless fountains of manhood, wasted, lavished. The paradox of a beaten army which gathers strength, a retreating host whose very withdrawal is fatal to the conquerors.

Our Russian money was running low, so in the morning we went out to change our English gold. But no one wanted English gold. Everybody asked the same question, in a low voice, peering around to see that no soldiers were within hearing: 'Have you any Austrian money?' For already it was rumoured in the city that the Austrians were coming again.

We kept our appointment with Troubetskoi, who led us through the ancient throne-room of the palace to the office of the governor-general's assistant, a pleasant-mannered officer whose coat blazed with decorations.

'Prince Troubetskoi and I have really done our best for you,' he said with a friendly smile. 'But the governor regrets that he cannot give you permission to visit the front. For that you must apply to the military authorities – he is simply a civil official, you know.... However, I haven't a doubt that they will allow you to go. And in that case, return here and we shall be most happy to take care of you.'

We asked where the permission was to be had.

'There are two ways. Either you may proceed to Petrograd, and arrange matters with his Highness the Grand Duke Nicolai Nicolaievitch through your ambassadors, or go to Cholm in Poland, which is the headquarters of General Ivanov, commander-in-chief of the southwestern front. Both Prince Troubetskoi and I think you will be more successful if you make application to General Ivanov, and his Excellency the governor-general is of the same opinion. I will give you passes which will carry you to Cholm.'

At midnight we left the hotel to catch the train for Cholm, and there being no cabs in sight, an officer bound for the station called out in French that he would be happy if we would share his. His oval, half-Semitic face might have been copied from an Assyrian wall-painting – he said he was a Georgian from the Caucasus.

'The Georgian regiments have been ordered here from the Turkish front, because of their heroic conduct. The Grand Duke has done right; we Georgians are by far the bravest soldiers in the army,' said he.

'Will the Austrians take Lemberg?' asked Robinson.

'Oh yes,' he answered complacently: 'We expect them every day now. But it doesn't matter, you know. Next winter we'll come back – or the winter after.'

Twelve
AN OPTIMISTIC PILGRIMAGE

Cholm is not a hundred miles in an airline from Lemberg, but there is no direct railroad between them; one must make a wide detour into Russia and back through Poland, more than three hundred miles.

We were in a compartment for four, the other two being a silent young lieutenant who lay in his berth with his boots on, smoking, and a crotchety old general invalided home. The general tried to shut tight both door and window – for the Russians share with other Continental peoples a morbid fear of fresh air. There followed a dramatic battle lasting all night, in which stalwart American manhood defied the liveried minions of the Tsar to close that window – but was finally subdued at dawn by the railroad police. . . .

White Russia. For hours we rode through an untouched wilderness of birch and pine without seeing a house or a human being, the engine's whistle alone breaking the echoing silence of the woods. Sometimes a gap in the forest gave glimpses of wide yellow plains, where black tree-stumps stood among the wheat. Wretched villages huddled around the government vodka shop – now closed – wooden huts roofed with neglected thatch, which straggled miserably beside muddy, rutted spaces populous with rooting pigs and immense flocks of geese. . . .

Great-shouldered women were working in the fields, mowing with broad strokes rhythmically abreast – probably some Female Mowers' Guild from a distant country. There were plenty of young, strong *mujiks* everywhere. They swung axes amid crashing-down trees, drove singing along the roads, and swarmed over the joists and timbers of giant miles of sheds that covered the mountainous heaps of army supplies. Yet not for an instant could we forget the war. The towns were all full of shouting soldiers; train after train whirled westward, packed with them. And as we paused on side-tracks, past glided an endless procession of white sanitary cars with pale, agonized faces peering from the windows under their bandages. Every village had its military hospital....

We changed trains at Rovno, where there was a wait of nine hours. There we ran into Miroshnikov, the English-speaking subofficer who had looked after us in Tarnopol, now bound north on official business.

'Let's walk around,' he proposed. 'I want to show you a typical Jewish town of the Pale.'

As we went along, I asked the meaning of the red, white, and blue cord that edged his shoulder-straps.

'That means I am a volunteer – exempt from compulsory service. The Russian word for "volunteer," ' he answered the question with a grin, 'is "*Volnoopredielyayoustchemusia.*" '

We gave up all hopes of learning the language....

I can never forget Rovno, the Jewish town of the Pale of Settlement. It was Russian in its shabby largeness, wide streets half paved with cobbles, dilapidated sidewalks, rambling wooden houses ornamented with scroll-saw trimmings painted bright green, and the swarming uniforms of its minor officialdom. Tiny-wheeled cabs abounded, with their heavy Russian yoke, driven by hairy degenerates who wore tattered velveteen robes and bell-top hats of outrageous shape. But all the rest was Jewish.... The street was heaped with evil-smelling rubbish, amid slimy puddles splashed up by every passing conveyance. Clouds of bloated flies buzzed about. On

95

both sides a multitude of little shops strangled each other, and their glaring signs, daubed with portraits of the articles for sale, made a crazy-quilt up and down as far as one could see. The greasy proprietors stood in their reeking doorways, each one bawling to us to buy from *him*, and not from his cheating competitor across the way. Too many shops, too many cab-drivers, barbers, tailors, herded into this narrow world where alone Jews are allowed to live in Russia; and periodically augmented with the miserable throngs cleared out from the forbidden cities, where they have bribed the police to stay. In the Pale a Jew gasps for breath indeed.

How different these were from even the poorest, meanest Jews in Galician cities. Here they were a pale, stooping, inbred race, refined to the point of idiocy. Cringing men with their 'sacred fringes' showing under their long coats – it was at Rovno that we first noticed the little peaked caps worn by Polish Jews – faintly bearded boys with unhealthy faces, girls prematurely aged with bitter work and eternal humiliation, grown women wrinkled and bent, in wigs and slovenly mother hubbards. People who smiled deprecatingly and hatefully when you looked at them, who stepped into the street to let Gentiles pass. And in the very centre of it all, a Russian church with blue incense pouring out the open door, a glitter of gold, jewels, and candle-lighted *ikons* within, priests in stoles heavy with woven gold threads, atremble with slow, noble chanting.

For a thousand years the Russians and their Church have done their best to exterminate the Jews and their religion. With what success? Here in Rovno were thousands of Jews shut in an impregnable world of their own, scrupulously observing a religion incessantly purified, practising their own customs, speaking their own language, with two codes of morals – one for each other and the other for the Gentiles. Persecution has only engendered a poison and a running sore in the body of the Russian people. It is true what Miroshnikov said, as we drank *kvass* in a little Jewish bar – that all Jews were traitors to Russia. Of course they are.

An officer whom we had met on the train came in. He sniffed the air, bowed to us, and staring malevolently at the frightened girls who served, said distinctly: 'The dirty Jews! I detest them!' and walked out.

We were around Rovno station almost all day long, but it was not until evening that the police decided to arrest us. Among others we appealed to a pompous colonel, named Bolatov, whom we had encountered several times in the course of our travels. He was covered with high decorations, carried a gold honour sword, and had padding in his chest and dye on his ferocious mustache. We never could discover what he did on his leisurely peregrinations around the country. Miroshnikov told him that Robinson was a celebrated artist.

'We shall see!' said Bolatov cunningly. He approached Robinson. 'If you are an artist,' said he, 'please draw my portrait.'

He struck a martial attitude under the arclight, chest expanded, hand on sword-hilt, and mustache twisted up, while Robinson drew for his life. The portrait was an outrageous flattery. Colonel Bolatov glanced at it with perfect satisfaction. He waved to the police.

'Release these gentlemen,' he ordered loftily. 'They are well-known journalists.... Would you mind signing this sketch?'

That night we slept on the benches of a troop-transport car; changed and waited seven hours at Kovel, and boarded a train bound eventually for Cholm, though no one knew when it would get there. All afternoon we crawled slowly westward through the great Polish plain – vast wheat-fields edged with a foam of red poppies, breaking like a yellow sea against cloudy promontories of trees, and archipelagoes of cheerful thatched villages. Half smothered in mighty blooming locusts were wooden stations where hospitable samovars steamed, and slow-moving heavy-faced peasants stared motionless at the train – the men in long grey coats of coarse wool, the women gay with bright-coloured skirts and kerchiefs. And late in the day when the low sun inundated the flat world with rich mellow light, and all the red, green, and yellow glowed vividly luminous, we whistled through a sandy pine wood, and saw before us the tree-covered hill of Cholm, with its cluster of shining Greek cupolas floating like golden bubbles above the green foliage.

A new-found but already intimate friend named Captain Martinev was criticising the army with true Russian candidness.

'– horrible waste,' said he. 'Let me tell you a story. In October I was with my regiment in Tilsit when the German drive on Warsaw began, and we received urgent orders to hurry to Poland. Well, from Tilsit to the nearest railroad station, Mittau, is a hundred versts. We did it in three days' forced marches, arriving in bad shape. Something had gone wrong – we had to wait twenty-four hours on the platform, without sleep, for it was very cold. By train we travelled two days to Warsaw, almost starving; no one had made arrangements for feeding us. When we arrived Lodz had already fallen. We got in at night and were marched across the city to another train bound for Teresa, where they were fighting. A little way out the tracks had been smashed by a shell; we detrained in the rain at two o'clock in the morning, and marched five hours to Teresa.

'At eight o'clock we reached the headquarters of the division commanded by General M –, who made such frightful mistakes in Manchuria. Our men's feet were in terrible condition; they had had practically no sleep for three nights, and hardly any food at all for two days.... Half an hour after we had thrown ourselves down exhausted in the rain, the general came out with his chief of staff.

' "How many men have I here?" he asked surlily.

' "Eight thousand."

' "Good. Send them to relieve the trenches."

'Our colonel protested. "But my men cannot go into the trenches. They must have rest and food. For five days –"

' "Never mind!" snapped the general. "I don't want your opinion. March!"

'The general went back to bed. We coaxed, pleaded, threatened, flogged – it was terrible to hear them beg for food and sleep – and the column staggered off to the forward trenches....

'We went in at ten in the morning and stood particularly heavy fire all day – so heavy that the cook-wagons couldn't reach us until midnight, so there was nothing to eat. The Germans attacked twice in the night, so there was no sleep. Next morning heavy artillery bombarded us. The men reeled as if they were drunk, forgot to take any precautions, and went to sleep while they were shooting. The officers, with blazing eyes, muttering things like men walking in their sleep, went up and down beating the soldiers with the flat of their swords.... I forgot what I was doing, and so did everybody, I think; indeed, I can't remember what followed at all – but we were in there for four days and four nights. Once a night the cook-wagons brought soup and bread. At least three times a night the Germans attacked at the point of the bayonet. We retired from trench to trench, turning like beasts at bay – though we were all out of our heads....

'Finally on the fifth morning they relieved us. Out of eight thousand men two thousand came back, and twelve hundred of those went to the hospital.

'But the amusing thing about it was that all the time we were being butchered out there, there were six fresh regiments held in reserve two miles away! What on earth do you suppose General M – was thinking of?'

Thirteen

THE FACE OF RUSSIA

Whoever has not travelled on the broad-gauge Russian rail-ways does not know the delights of great cars half as wide again as American cars, berths too long and too ample, ceil-ings so high that you can stand in the upper berth. The train takes its smooth-rolling, leisurely way, drawn by wood-burning locomotives belching sweet-smelling birch smoke and showers of sparks, stopping long at little stations where there are always good restaurants. At every halt boys bring trays of tea glasses through the train, sandwiches, sweet cakes, and cigarettes. There are no specified hours for arriving anywhere, no fixed times for eating or sleeping. Often on a journey I have seen the dining-car come on at midnight, and everybody go in and have dinner with interminable conversation, lasting until time for breakfast. One man rents bedclothes from the porter, and disrobes in full view of the rest of the company in his compartment; others turn in on the bare mattresses; and the rest sit up drinking eternal *chai* and endlessly arguing. Windows are shut and doors. One stifles in thick cigarette smoke, and there are snores from the upper berth, and con-tinual movement of persons getting up, going to bed, drifting in and out.

In Russia every one talks about his soul. Almost any con-versation might have been taken from the pages of a Dos-toievsky novel. The Russians get drunk on their talk; voices ring, eyes flash, they are exalted with a passion of self-revelation. In Petrograd I have seen a crowded café at two o'clock in the morning – of course no liquor was to be had – shouting and singing and pounding on the tables, quite intoxicated with ideas.

Outside the windows of the train the amazing country flows by, flat as a table; for hours the ancient forest marches, alongside, leagues and leagues of it, untouched by the axe, mysterious and sombre. At the edge of the trees runs a dusty track along which an occasional heavy cart lumbers, its rough-coated horse surmounted by a great wooden yoke from which dangles a brass bell, the driver a great-shouldered *mujik* with a brutish face overhung with hair. Hours apart are little thatched towns, mere slashings in the primeval woods, built of untrimmed boards around the wooden church, with its bright-painted cupolas, and the government vodka shop – closed now – easily the most pretentious building in the village. Wooden sidewalks on stilts, unpaved alley-like streets that are sloughs of mud, immense piles of cord-wood to burn in the engine – for all the world like a railroad town in the timber of the great Northwest. Immense women with gay-coloured kerchiefs around their hair and dazzling teeth, booted giants of men in peaked caps and whiskers, and priests in long, black coats and stovepipe hats with brims. Along the platform, tall policemen much in evidence, with their yellow blouses, scarlet revolver cords, and swords. Soldiers, of course, everywhere – by the tens of thousands.... Then great fields breaking suddenly from the woods and stretching to the far horizon, golden-heavy with wheat with black stumps sticking up in it.

Russians are not patriotic like other races, I think. The Tsar to them is not the head of the government; he is a divinity. The government itself – the bureaucracy – commands no loyalty from the masses; it is like a separate nation imposed upon the Russian people. As a rule, they do not know what their flag looks like, and if they do it is not the symbol of

Russia. And the Russian national hymn is a hymn, a half-mystical great song; but no one feels it necessary to rise and remove his hat when it is played. As a people, they have no sympathy with imperialism – they do not wish to make Russia a great country by conquest – in fact, they do not seem to realize that there is any world outside of Russia; that is why they fight so badly on an invasion of the enemy's country. But once let the enemy set foot on Russian soil, and the *mujiks* turn into savage beasts, as they did in 1812 and in 1915. Their farms, their houses, the woods and plains and holy cities are under the heel of the foreigner; that is why they fight so well on defence.

Russians seem to have a Greek feeling for the land, for the wide flat plains, the deep forests, the mighty rivers, the tremendous arch of sky that is over Russia, the churches incrusted with gold and jewels, where countless generations of their fathers have touched the ikons, for the tremendous impulses that set whole villages wandering in search of a sacred river, for the cruel hardness of the northern winter, for the fierce love and the wild gaiety, and the dreadful gloom, and the myths and legends which are Russia. Once a young officer travelled with us in our compartment, and all day long he gazed out of the window at the dark woods, the vast fields, the little towns, and tears rolled down his cheeks. 'Russia is a mighty mother; Russia is a mighty mother,' he said over and over again. . . .

Another time it was a middle-aged civilian with a bullet head shaved close, and wide, staring, light-blue eyes that gave him the expression of a mystic.

'We Russians do not know how great we are,' he said. 'We cannot grasp the idea of so many millions of people to communicate with. We do not realize how much land, how much riches we have. Why, I can tell you of one, Mr Yousoupov of Moscow, who owns more land than he knows, whose estates are greater than the territory of any German

King. And no Russian realizes how many races are embraced in this nation; I myself know only thirty-nine. . . .'

Yet this vast chaotic agglomeration of barbarian races, brutalized and tyrannized over for centuries, with only the barest means of intercommunication, without consciousness of any one ideal, has developed a profound national unity of feeling and thought and an original civilization that spreads by its own power. Loose and easy and strong, it invades the life of the far-flung savage tribes of Asia; it crosses the frontiers into Rumania, Galicia, East Prussia – in spite of organized efforts to stop it. Even the English, who usually cling stubbornly to their way of living in all countries and under all conditions, are overpowered by Russia; the English colonies in Moscow and Petrograd are half Russian. And it takes holds of the minds of men because it is the most comfortable, the most liberal way of life. Russian ideas are the most exhilarating, Russian thought the freest, Russian art the most exuberant; Russian food and drink are to me the best, and Russians themselves are, perhaps, the most interesting human beings that exist.

They have a sense of space and time which fits them. In America we are the possessors of a great empire – but we live as if this were a crowded island like England, where our civilization came from. Our streets are narrow and our cities congested. We live in houses crushed up against one another, or in apartments, layer on layer; each family a little shut-in-cell, self-centred and narrowly private. Russia is also a great empire; but there the people live as if they knew it were one. In Petrograd some streets are a quarter-mile broad and there are squares three-quarters of a mile across, and buildings whose façades run on uninterrupted for half a mile. Houses are always open; people are always visiting each other at all hours of the day and night. Food and tea and conversation flow interminably; every one acts just as he feels like acting, and says just what he wants to. There are no particular times for getting up or going to bed or eating dinner, and there is no conventional way of murdering a man, or of making love. To most people a Dostoievsky novel reads like the chronicle of an insane asylum; but that, I think, is because the Russians are not restrained by the traditions and conventions that rule the social conduct of the rest of the world.

This is not only true of the great cities but of the small towns, and even the villages as well. The Russian peasant cannot be taught to tell time by the clock. He is so close to the earth, so much a part of it, that machine-made time means nothing to him. But he must be regular, or his crops will not grow; so he ploughs and plants and reaps by rain, wind, snow, and the march of the seasons – and he lives according to the sun, moon, and stars. Once the peasant is driven into the cities to work in the factories he loses the driving compulsion of nature, and when he has risen above the necessity of factory hours, there is no further reason for him to live a regular life.

We saw something of life in a Russian household; samovars perpetually steaming, servants shuffling in and out with fresh water and fresh tea-leaves, laughing and joining in the perpetual clatter of conversation. In and out flowed an unbroken stream of relatives, friends, comparative strangers. There was always tea, always a long sideboard heaped with *zakouska*, always a hundred little groups telling stories, loudly arguing, laughing uproariously, always little parties of card-players. Meals occurred whenever anybody got hungry – or rather there was a perpetual meal going on. Some went to bed, others rose after a long sleep and had breakfast. Day and night it never seemed to stop.

And in Petrograd we knew some people who received callers between eleven o'clock at night and dawn. Then they went to bed, and did not get up again until evening. For three years they hadn't seen daylight – except in the white nights of summer. Many interesting characters went there; among them an old Jew who had bought immunity from the police for years, and who confided to us that he had written a history of Russian political thought in five volumes; four volumes had appeared, and had been regularly confiscated upon publication – he was now engaged upon the fifth. He was always discussing politics in a loud voice, breaking off every now and then to look out of the window to see if there were any police listening. For he had been in jail once for speaking the word 'socialism.' Before he began to talk he would take us into a corner and in a whisper explain that when he said 'daisy,' that meant 'socialism'; and when he said 'poppy,' that meant 'revolution.' And then he would go ahead, striding up and down the room, and shouting all sorts of destructive doctrines.

For the Russia of melodrama and of the English popular magazines still exists. I remember seeing some prisoners on the platform of a station where our train stopped. They were huddled between the tracks: two or three young stupid-looking *mujiks* with cropped heads, a bent old man half-blind, a Jew or so, and some women, one a mere girl with a baby. Around them was a ring of police with bared swords.

'Where are they going?' I asked the conductor.

'Siberia,' he whispered out of the corner of his mouth.

'What have they done?'

'Don't ask questions,' he snapped nervously. 'If you ask questions in Russia *that* is what happens to you!'

There were some preposterous war regulations in Petrograd. If you spoke German over the telephone you were subject to a fine of three thousand roubles, and if you were heard talking German on the street the penalty was Siberia. I have it on very good authority that two professors of Oriental languages were walking down the Morskaia, speaking ancient Armenian to each other, they were arrested, and the police swore that it was German. And from that day to this they have never again been heard of.

In spite of this, however, the fact remains that any German

THE WAR IN EASTERN EUROPE

with money could go on living in Petrograd or Moscow, and
manifest his patriotism in any way he pleased. For instance,
the large German colony of Moscow gave a dinner in the city's
most fashionable hotel during November, 1914, at which
German songs were chanted, addresses in German delivered
which consigned the Tsar and his allies to purgatory, and
shouts of 'Hoch der Kaiser!' rent the air. Nothing whatever
was done about this; but six months later the police determined to teach them a lesson without appearing at all prominent – which would have cut off their German revenues.
Quantities of vodka were dug up from somewhere, the ikons
taken from the churches, and, encouraged by the police, the
mob started out to wreck German houses, shops, and hotels.
After the first few of these had been demolished the people
turned their attention to the French, English, and Russian
establishments, shouting: 'Down with the rich! You have
speculated too long with our money!' Before the riot ended
almost every great store in Moscow had been smashed and
pillaged, and many wealthy Russians, men and women, torn
from their automobiles and carriages and thrown into the
canal. The Russian people of the upper classes did not disdain
to take advantage of the situation. They sent their footmen
and valets down to plunge into the riot, and take whatever
silks and laces and furs they could lay their hands on.... As
a consequence of this patriotic demonstration, the governor
of the city, the governor of the province, and the chief of
police were discharged from office.

How the Germans were finally removed from Moscow, is
another characteristic tale of Russian methods. Did they
banish them? Did they put them in detention camps? No. The
police let it privately be known that if the Moscow Germans
wished to leave Russia, there was a means. In Moscow, they
said, it was impossible for a German to get a passport to return
to his own country; but if he would go to the government of
Perm, on the edge of Siberia at the base of the Ural Mountains,

he could there apply for a passport and be allowed to leave. Hundreds of Germans took the hint and crowded the trains that went in the direction of Perm. They are still there.

There are four distinct sets of Russian secret police, and their main job is to supervise the regular police and to spy upon each other, besides the *dvorniks*, who act as *concierges* at your front door, and are all members of the government detective force. In times like the present, particularly, a mere suspicion is enough to send you to a military court martial, unless you have influence, or to spirit you away to Siberia.

Fourteen

PETROGRAD AND MOSCOW

Most travellers speak of Moscow as the Heart of Russia the real Russian city, and dismiss Petrograd as an imitation of other European capitals. But to me Petrograd seems more characteristically Russian – with its immense façades of government buildings and barracks marching along as far as the eye can reach, broad streets, and mighty open spaces. The great stone quays along the Neva, the palaces, cathedrals, and Imperial avenues paved with cobbles grew under the hands of innumerable serfs chained in a swamp by the will of a tyrant, and were cemented with their blood; for where Petrograd now sprawls for miles and miles, a city built for giants, was nothing but a feverish marsh a hundred and fifty years ago. And there, where no roads naturally lead, the most desolate spot, the most vulnerable and the most remote from any natural centre of the Russian Empire, Peter the Great had a whim to found his capital. Twenty thousand workmen a year for ten years were killed by fever, cold, and disease in the building of Petrograd. Nine times the court nobles themselves conspired to wreck the hated city and force the court to return to Moscow; three times they set fire to it, and three times the Tsar hung them at the doors of the palaces he had forced them to build. A powerful section of the Reactionary party has always agitated for the restoration of Moscow as capital, and it is only in the last twenty years that the population of Petrograd has not been artificially kept up.

Great canals of deep, sombre water curve through the city everywhere, and along these move vast wooden barges hundreds of feet long, piled high with birch-wood for burning – cut in the gloom of ancient forests with ringing axes, and floated down flat, deserted rivers to the sound of slow minor boat songs under the northern lights. And into the dark water every night obscure and restless, miserable poor throw themselves – multitudes of them. Their bodies go out with the tide, under the frowning interminable barracks, slipping through the caves beneath the streets, and float to sea on the broad Neva along that splendid front of palaces yellow and barbarically red, those fantastic cupolas and pinnacles and gigantic monuments.

In the immense silent squares and wide streets the people are lost; in spite of its two millions or more of human beings Petrograd seems perpetually empty. Only on summer evenings, in the enormous amusement parks, among the open-air theatres, scenic railways, merry-go-rounds, and cafés, hundreds of thousands of people, in great masses and currents of shouting, laughing, singing humanity, move aimlessly to and fro, with a feeling of uncontrollable force like the sea. Or in time of revolution, or during some important religious festival, when the people choke miles of great streets from wall to wall, and the thunder of their untimed feet, the roar of their unorganized singing, the power of their spontaneous will dwarfs even that Imperial City.

On the day of the fiesta of Our Lady of Kazan I was caught at the corner of the Nevski Prospekt and the Morskaia by sudden inundations of great mobs pouring toward the cathedral from every street, hats off, faces exultingly raised, deep voices lifting simple slow hymns. Over their heads swam the jewelled and glittering ikons, upheld by bareheaded, bearded giant priests in rich vestments all covered with gold. Small choir-boys swung censers. Flanking the holy procession, peasant women walked sideways, hand in hand, with blank exalted faces, guarding the ikons. Men and women crowded in single file to pass under the sacred images, screaming, kicking, and pulling each other; and every few minutes the priests lowered them while a hundred kneeling people flung themselves forward to kiss the pictures with their lips. And all the time the processions moved slowly on in that terrible sea of people, meeting, crossing, wavering over the heads of the crowd, flashing back the sun that burst out between clouds. And for hours a solid mile and a half of people blocked the Nevski Prospekt and all the streets adjoining before the Cathedral of Our Lady of Kazan, praying and crossing themselves with a fluttering motion, and singing.

With Russians religion is extraordinarily alive. On the streets people cross themselves incessantly, especially when passing the churches, and the cab-drivers lift their hats and touch forehead, breast, and shoulders whenever they see an ikon. Little chapels are open all day long, even in the fashionable shopping quarters, and there are continual services for the constantly flowing crowds that stop to kneel and kiss the holy images as they pass. In certain very holy churches and shrines there is always, day and night, a jam of people, kneeling, bowing, muttering before the *ikonostas*. But, as far as I could discover, religion in Russia does not seem to be a temporal power, or a matter of politics, or a moral or ethical rule of life. The priests have often mean, vicious faces, and monks in the great monasteries lead the extravagantly dissolute lives of rich and unrestrained ecclesiastics everywhere; and the church, like all powerful churches, lives fatly and builds its golden altar-screens from the contributions of the poor, by playing on their darkest superstitions. To the simple Russian peasant, however, his religion is a source of spiritual force, both a divine blessing on his undertakings and a mystical communion with God. The thief and the murderer go to kiss the ikons before robbing a house or killing a man. The revolutionists carry the ikons at the head of their ranks, and the mobs that shoot them down also have ikons. In every Russian house an ikon hangs in the corner of the room, and in every hotel and railway-station.

Great religious fervours shake the Russian people, as they did the Jews and the Arabs, splitting them into innumerable mystical sects. Miracles occur frequently; holy men and self-torturing saints wander about the country, healing and preaching strange gospels. Even in Petrograd, the least religious of Russian cities, priests and monks were everywhere, and one of them, Gregory Rasputin, was rumoured to be almost the real ruler of the empire.

At night – for it was June – the sun sank slower and slower. At nine o'clock it was as light as late summer evenings at home; at half past ten the sun touched the horizon, and moved slowly around from west to east until half past two in the morning, when it rose again. If you happened to wake up at midnight it was impossible to tell whether it was night or day – especially since the Russians seemed to have no regular hours for going to bed. Outside our window in St Isaac's Square people would be sitting on the benches reading their newspapers; before the house doors squatted the *dvorniks* huddled in their *shubas*, gossiping; cabs drove past, and people went along the sidewalk, and there were even shops open.

Sometimes we drove. *'Istvosschik!'* I cried, standing in the middle of the street, and immediately there materialized from nowhere twenty or thirty little cabs driven by hairy individuals crowned with glazed, bell-shaped hats with curling brims, and padded under their coats so as to appear monstrously fat. Driving round and round us, they screamed hideously their competitive prices. There was a municipal tariff for cabs, and a copy of it was posted on the back of the driver's seat; but you had to pay at least double the prices on it. And the police always took the cabman's part.

We roamed around the city in the interminable twilight. In

front of the barracks dense little crowds surrounded some soldier leaping and kicking on his hams a peasant dance, perhaps from Siberia, to the breathless braying of an accordion. In St Isaac's Square the new recruits by companies were stamping through their drill, with resounding great boots, and roaring the traditional regimental answers to the greeting of a general.

'Good morning, my children!' cried a high, flat voice.

'Good morning to your Generalship!' bellowed a hundred big men in unison.

'I congratulate you, my children!'

'Happy to have had the opportunity, your Generalship!'

Three or four times a day the bell-ringers in the ponderous cupolas of St Isaac's Cathedral looped the bell-ropes about their elbows, knees, feet, and hands, and all the great and little bells began to boom and jangle – thirty-five of them – in a wild, dissonant ragtime:

Teeng! Tong! Teeng-ting-a-tang-tong! Boom! Bom-tick-a-ting-tingle-ingle-boom!   Tang-tong-tick-a-tangle-tongle-boom-tang-tingle-tick-tick-a-bom!

By hundreds, by thousands the new recruits, still in their peasant clothes, with big numbers chalked on their backs, passed by. There seemed no end to them. Day after day and week after week they poured into Petrograd, and had been pouring in for more than a year, to be roughly whipped into shape, loaded on endless trains, and hurled carelessly westward or south to choke with the slaughter of sheer numbers the terrible German machine.... And yet everywhere on the streets, and all over Russia, I saw multitudes of fresh men who have not yet been called to the colours.

Moscow, known affectionately to all Russians as *Matuschka Moskva*, 'Little Mother Moscow,' is still the Holy City, the intellectual capital, and the last stronghold of the old splendid barbaric Russia. Moscow's streets are narrow, and her cities crowd wall within wall around the sacred citadel which epitomizes all the history of the empire. But the pulse of Russia and the red renewing blood and the flow of change have left Moscow. Her ancient and opulent commerce, however, that made Muscovite merchant princes a legend in Europe in the Middle Ages, is still growing. The number of buildings of modern German architecture strikes one immediately.

That wideness and vastness and lavish disregard of human life so characteristic of Petrograd, of the war, and of Russia as it seemed to me, again appears in the Kremlin, where for a thousand years the hopes and the longings and the faith of the Russian people were centred. The Red Square is as gigantic as any square in the new capital, and immeasurably ancient. Cyclopean red walls, crenellated and topped with fantastic towers, pierced with gates in whose gloom hang great staring ikons, stride down-hill, and along the bank of the river, proudly encircling the most insolently rich capitol in the world. Inside, upon one square, within a hundred yards of each other, stand four cathedrals, each with an altar-screen of solid gold and jewels, glittering up from the long ranks of the tombs of Tsars, into the cloud of blue incense that forever palls a ceiling inlaid with monstrous mosaics. Ivan Veliki leans upward, honeycombed with great bells. Miles of palaces twist and turn, whose rooms are furnished in solid slabs of gold and pillars of semiprecious stones – Imperial throne-room after throne-room, to the gaudy, half-savage apartments where Ivan the Terrible lived, and the treasury that holds the Peacock Throne of Persia, and the Golden Throne of the Tartars, and the Diamond Throne of the Tsars. Monasteries, barracks, ancient arsenals along whose façades are piled the thousands of cannon that Napoleon left on the road from Moscow; the huge bell of Boris Godounov cracked and lying on the ground; the Tsar cannon, too big for any charge – and out through the Spasskya Gate, with the soldiers on guard to see that you remove your hat when you pass under the Ikon of the Redeemer....

On Sunday we took the steamer up the river to the Sparrow Hills, where Napoleon stood to watch Moscow burning. Along the river for miles people were bathing from the bank, groups of men and women, and all over the hills swarmed an immense multitude making holiday. They sprawled on the grass, ran races, moved in big singing droves under the trees; and in little hollows and flat places accordions jiggled, while the wild stamping dances went on. There were drunken people haranguing huge audiences, and senseless men asleep, clutching bottles in their hands, and cripples and idiots followed by laughing throngs, like a mediæval fair. An old woman in rags came hobbling down the hill, her hair streaming about her face, lifted arms with clenched fists over her head, shouting hysterically. A man and a girl pounded each other with their fists, weeping. On a high point of land stood a soberly dressed man with his hands clasped behind his back, evidently making a speech to the restless flowing crowds beneath him. There was in the air a feeling of recklessness and gloom, as if anything might happen....

We sat a long time in the café at the top of the hill, looking out over the plain where the river made a great curve, while the sun sank westward over the innumerable bulbs and cupolas of golden, green, blue, pink, and clashing colours of the four hundred churches of Moscow. And as we sat there, far, faintly, and wild came the galloping clangour of countless bells, beating out the rhythm that has in it all the deep solemnity and mad gaiety of Russia.

Fifteen

TOWARD THE CITY OF EMPERORS

The handsome great sleeping-cars bore brass inscriptions in *svelte* Turkish letters and in French, 'Orient Express' – that most famous train in the world, which used to run from Paris direct to the Golden Horn in the prehistoric days before the war. A sign in Bulgarian said 'Tsarigrad' – literally 'City of Emperors' – also the Russian name for the eastern capital that all Slavs consider theirs by right. And a German placard proclaimed pompously, 'Berlin-Constantinopel' – an arrogant prophecy in those days, when the Constantinople train went no farther west than Sofia, and the drive on Serbia had not begun.

We were an international company: Three English officers in mufti bound for Dedeagatch; a French engineer on business to Philipopolis; a Bulgar military commission going to discuss the terms of the treaty with Turkey; a Russian school-teacher returning to his home in Burgas; an American tobacco man on a buying tour around the Turkish Black Sea ports; a black eunuch in fez, his frock coat flaring over wide hips and knock knees; a Viennese music-hall dancer and her man headed for the café concerts of Pera; two Hungarian Red Crescent delegates, and assorted Germans to the number of about a hundred. There was a special car full of bullet-headed Krupp workmen for the Turkish munition factories, and two compartments reserved for an *Unterseeboot* crew going down to relieve the men of U-54 – boys seventeen or eighteen years old. And in the next compartment to mine a party of seven upper-class Prussians played incessant 'bridge': government officials, business men, and intellectuals on their way to Constantinople to take posts in the embassy, the Regie, the Ottoman Debt, and the Turkish universities. Each was a highly efficient cog, trained to fit exactly his place in the marvellous German machine that ground already for the Teutonic Empire of the East.

The biting irony of life in neutral countries went with us. It was curious to watch the ancient habit of cosmopolitan existence take possession of that train-load. Some ticket agent with a sense of humour had paired two Englishmen with a couple of German embassy attachés in the same compartment – they were scrupulously polite to each other. The Frenchman and the other Britisher gravitated naturally to the side of the fair Austrian, where they all laughed and chattered about youthful student days in Vienna. Late at night I caught one of the German diplomats out in the corridor gossiping about Moscow with the Russian teacher. All these men were active on the firing-line, so to speak, except the Russian – and he, of course, was a Slav, and without prejudices....

But in the morning the English, the Frenchman, and the Russian were gone – the breathing-place between borders of hate was past – and we fled through the grim marches of the Turkish Empire.

The shallow, sluggish, yellow Maritza River, bordered by gigantic willows, twisted through an arid valley. Dry, brown hills rolled up, on whose slopes no green thing grew; flat plains baked under scanty scorched grass; straggly corn-fields lay drooping, with roofed platforms on stilts starting up here and there, where black-veiled women squatted with guns across their knees to scare away the crows. Rarely a village – miserable huts of daubed mud, thatched with dirty straw, clustering around the flat dome of a little mosque and its shabby minaret. Westward, a mile away, the ruins of a red-tiled town climbed the hillside, silent and deserted since the Bulgarians bombarded it in 1912, and shot off the tips of the two minarets. The crumbling stumps of minarets stood alone on the desolate flats, marking the spot of some once-living village or town whose very traces had disappeared – so quickly do the ephemeral buildings of the Turks return to the dust; but the minarets stand, for it is forbidden to demolish a mosque that has once been consecrated.

Sometimes we stopped at a little station; a group of huts, a minaret, adobe barracks, and rows of mud-bricks baking in the sun. A dozen gayly painted little *arabas* slung high on their springs waited for passengers; six or seven veiled women would crowd into one, pull the curtains to shield them from the public gaze, and rattle giggling away in a cloud of golden dust. Bare-legged peasant *hanums*, robed all in dull green, shuffled single file along the road, carrying naked babies, with a coquettish lifting of veils for the windows of the train. By the platform were piled shimmering heaps of melons brought from the interior – the luscious green sugar-melon, and the yellow *kavoon*, which smells like flowers and tastes like nothing else in the world. An ancient tree beside the station spread an emerald shade over a tiny café, where the turbaned, slippered old Turks of the country sat gravely at their coffee and *narghilehs*.

Along the railway, aged bent peasants, unfit for the firing-line, stood guard – barefooted, ragged, armed with rusty hammer-lock muskets and belted with soft-nosed bullets of an earlier vintage still. They made a pathetic effort to straighten up in military attitudes as we passed.... But it was at Adrianople that we saw the first regular Turkish soldiers, in their unfitting khaki uniforms, puttees, and those German-designed soft helmets that look like Arab turbans, and come down flat on the forehead, so that a Mohammedan can salaam in prayers without uncovering. A mild-faced, serious, slow-moving people they seemed.

The brisk young Prussian who got on at Adrianople was strikingly different. He wore the uniform of a Bey in the Turkish army, with a tall cap of brown astrakhan ornamented with the gold crescent, and on his breast were the ribbons of the Iron Cross, and the Turkish Order of the Hamidieh. His scarred face was set in a violent scowl, and he strode up and down the corridor, muttering *'Gottverdammte Dummheit!'* from time to time. At the first stop he descended, looked sharply around, and barked something in Turkish to the two tattered old railway guards who were scuffling along the platform.

'Tchabouk! Hurry!' he snapped. 'Sons of pigs, hurry when I call!'

Startled, they came running at a stiff trot. He looked them up and down with a sneer; then shot a string of vicious words at them. The two old men trotted off and, wheeling, marched stiffly back, trying to achieve the goose-step and salute in Prussian fashion. Again he bawled insultingly in their faces; again, with crestfallen expression, they repeated the manœuvre. It was ludicrous and pitiable to watch....

'Gott in Himmel!' cried the instructor to the world in general, shaking his fists in the air, 'were there ever such animals? Again! Again! *Tchabouk!* Run, damn you!'

Meanwhile, the other soldiers and the peasants had withdrawn from range, and stood in clusters at a distance, mildly inspecting this amazing human phenomenon.... Of a sudden a little Turkish corporal detached himself from the throng, marched up to the Prussian, saluted, and spoke. The other glared, flushed to his hair, the cords stood out on his neck, and he thrust his nose against the little man's nose, and screamed at him.

'Bey *effendi* –' began the corporal. And 'Bey *effendi* –' he tried again to explain. But the Bey went brighter scarlet, grew more offensive, and finally drew back in good old Prussian fashion and slapped him in the face. The Turk winced and then stood quite still, while the red print of a hand sprang out on his cheek, staring without expression straight into the other's eyes. Undefinable, scarcely heard, a faint wind of sound swept over all those watching people. . . .

All afternoon we crawled southeast through a blasted land. The low, hot air was heavy, as if with the breath of unnumbered generations of dead; a sluggish haze softened the distance. Thin corn-fields, irregular melon patches, dusty willows around a country well were all the vegetation. Occasionally there was a rustic thrashing-floor, where slow oxen drew round and round over the yellow corn a heavy sledge full of laughing, shouting youngsters. Once a caravan of shambling dromedaries, roped together, crossed our vision, rocking along with great dusty bales slung from their humps – the three small boys who were drivers skylarking about them. No living thing for miles and miles, nor any human evidences except the ruins of old cities, abandoned as the ebbing population withdrew into the city or Asia Minor beyond. . . . And yet this land has always been empty and desolate as it is to-day; even at the height of the Byzantine Empire, it was good policy to keep a barren waste between the City and the countries of the restless barbarians. . . .

Now we began to pass troop-trains. English submarines in the Sea of Marmora had paralyzed water transport to Gallipoli, and the soldiers went by railroad to Kouleli Gourgas, and then marched overland to Bulair. The freight-car doors were crowded with dark, simple faces; there came to us incessant quavering nasal singing to the syncopated accompaniment of shrill pipes and drums. One was full of savage-eyed Arabs from the desert east of Aleppo, dressed still in sweeping grey and brown burnooses, their thin, intense faces more startling for the encircling folds.

Tchataldja was feverishly active; narrow-gauge little trains loaded with guns, steel trench roofs, piles of tools, puffed off along the folds of the hills, and the naked, brown slopes swarmed with a multitude of tiny figures working on trenches against the eventuality of Bulgarian invasion....

The sun set behind, warming for an instant with a wash of gold the desolate leagues on leagues of waste. Night came suddenly, a moonless night of overwhelming stars. We moved slower and slower, waiting interminably on switches while the whining, singing troop-trains flashed by.... Toward midnight I fell asleep, and woke hours later to find one of the Germans shaking me.

'Constantinople,' said he.

I could make out the dim shape of a gigantic wall rushing up as we roared through a jagged breach in it. On the right crumbling half-battlements – the Byzantine sea-wall – fell suddenly away, and showed the sea lapping with tiny waves at the railway embankment; the other side was a rank of tall, unpainted wooden houses leaning crazily against each other, over mouths of gloom which were narrow streets, and piling back up the rising hill of the city in chaotic masses of jumbled roofs. Over these suddenly sprang out against the stars the mighty dome of an imperial mosque, minarets that soared immeasurably into the sky like great lances, broken masses of trees on Seraglio Point, with a glimpse of the steep black wall that had buttressed the Acropolis of the Greeks upon its mountain, the vague forms of kiosks, spiked chimneys of the imperial kitchens in a row, and the wide, flat roof of the Old Seraglio palace – Istamboul, the prize of the world.

Sixteen

CONSTANTINOPLE UNDER THE GERMANS

At four hours precisely, Turkish time (or three minutes past nine *à la fraqnue*), on the morning of *chiharshenbi, yigirmi utch* of the month of *Temoos*, year of the Hegira *bin utch yuze otouz utch*, I woke to an immense lazy roar, woven of incredibly varied noises – the indistinct shuffling of a million slippers, shouts, bellows, high, raucous peddler voices, the nasal wail of a *muezzin* strangely calling to prayer at this unusual hour, dogs howling, a donkey braying, and, I suppose, a thousand schools in mosque courtyards droning the Koran. From my balcony I looked down on the roofs of tall Greek apartments which clung timorously to the steep skirts of Pera and broke into a dark foam of myriad Turkish houses that rushed across the valley of Kassim Pasha, swirling around the clean white mosque and two minarets, and the wave of close trees they sprang from. The little houses were all wood – rarely with a roof of old red tiles – unpainted, weathered to a dull violet, clustered where the builder's caprice had set them, threaded with a maze of wriggling streets, and spotted with little windows that caught the sun – golden. Beyond the valley they crowded up the hillside, jumbled at every conceivable angle, like a pile of children's blocks – and all of the windows ablaze. Piale Pasha Mosque started up northward, dazzling, its minaret leaping from the very dome – built to look like the mast of a ship by the great Kaptan Pasha, who broke the sea power of Venice in the sixteenth century.

Down this valley Mohammed the Conqueror dragged his ships after hauling them over the high ridge where Pera stands, and launched them in the Golden Horn. Shabby Greek San Dimitri to the right; a dark pageant of cypresses along the crest over Kassim Pasha, that bounds the barren field of the *Ok-Meidan*, whose white stones mark the record shots of great Sultans who were masters of the bow and arrow; the heights of Haskeui, sombre with spacious wooden houses weathered black, where the great Armenian money princes lived in the dangerous days, and where now the Jews spawn in indescribable filth; northward again, over the mighty shoulder of a bald hill, the treeless, thick-clustered field of the Hebrew cemetery, as terrible as a razed city.

Bounding all to the west, the Golden Horn curved, narrowing east, around to north, a sheet of molten brass on which were etched black the Sultan's yacht and the yacht of the Khedive of Egypt – with the blue sphinxes painted on her stern – and the steamer *General*, sleeping quarters of German officers; dismantled second-rate cruisers, the pride of the Turkish navy, long gathering barnacles in the Golden Horn; the little cruiser *Hamedieh*, swarming with tiny dots, which were German sailors in fezzes; and countless swarms of darting *caïks*, like water-beetles.

Up from that bath of gold swept Stamboul from her clustering tangle of shanties on piles, rising in a pattern of huddling little roofs too intricate for any eye to follow, to the jagged crest lifting like music along her seven hills, where the great domes of the imperial mosques soared against the sky and flung aloft their spear-like minarets.

I could see the Stamboul end of the Inner Bridge and a little corner of the Port of Commerce, with the tangled jam of ships which were caught there when the war broke out. Above the bridge lay Phanar, where the Patriarch, who still signs himself 'Bishop of New Rome,' has his palace, for centuries the powerful fountain of life and death for all the millions of '*Roum-mileti*'; Phanar, refuge of imperial Byzantine families after the fall of the city, home of those merchant princes who astounded Renaissance Europe with their wealth and bad taste; Phanar, for five hundred years centre of the Greek race under the Turk. Farther along Balata – the Palatium of the Romans – and Aivan Serai above it, shadowed in the immense sprawling ruins of Byzantine palaces, where the walls of Manuel Commenus stagger up from the water and are lost in the city. Beyond, Eyoub, the sacred village of tombs around that dazzling mosque which no Christian may enter, and the interminable mass of cypresses of that holiest of all cemeteries, climbing the steep hill behind. Greek and Roman walls; the spikes of four hundred minarets; mosques that were built with a king's treasure in a burst of vanity by the old magnificent Sultans, others that were Christian churches under the Empress Irene, whose walls are porphyry and alabaster, and whose mosaics, whitewashed over, blaze through in gold and purple splendour; fragments of arches and columns of semiprecious stones, where once the golden statues of emperors stood – and marching splendidly across the sky-line of the city the double-arches of the tree-crowned aqueduct.

The hotel porter was a clever Italian with a nose for tips. He bent over me deferentially as I breakfasted, rubbing his hands.

'Excellency,' he said in French, 'the secret police have been here to inquire about your Excellency. Would your Excellency like me to tell them any particular thing...?'

Daoud Bey was waiting for me, and together we went out into Tramway Street, where the electric cars clang past, newsboys shout the late editions of the newspapers written in French – and apartment-houses, curiosity-shops, cafés, banks, and embassies look like a shabby quarter in an Italian city. Here every one, men and women, wore European clothes, just a trifle off in fashion, fit, and cloth – like 'store clothes' bought on Third Avenue. It was a crowd of no nations and of all bloods, clever, facile, unscrupulous, shallow – Levantine. At the gates of the few open embassies sat the conventional Montenegrin doorkeepers, in savage panoply of wide trousers and little jackets, and enormous sashes stuck full of pistols; *kavases* of consulates and legations slouched around the doors of diplomats, in uniforms covered with gold lace, fezzes with arms blazing on them, and swords. An occasional smart carriage went by, with driver and footmen wearing the barbaric livery of the diplomatic service. Yet turn into any street off the Grand Rue or the Rue des Tramways, and the tall overhanging buildings echoed with appeals of half-naked ladies leaning callously from windows all the way up to the fourth floor. In those narrow, twisting alleys the fakers and the thieves and the vicious and unfit of the Christian Orient crowded and shouted and passed; filth was underfoot, pots of ambiguous liquids rained carelessly down, and the smells were varied and interesting. Miles and miles of such streets, whole quarters given over to a kind of weak debauch; and fronting the cultivated gentlemen and delicate ladies of the European colony only the bold front of the shell of hotels and clubs and embassies.

It was the day after Warsaw fell into German hands. Yesterday the German places had hoisted the German and Turkish flags to celebrate the event. As we walked down the steep street, that with the mercilessness of modern civilization cuts an ancient Turkish cemetery in half so the street-cars may pass, Daoud Bey related interesting details of what followed.

'The Turkish police went around,' said he with some gusto, 'and ordered the German flags pulled down. We had the devil of a row, for the German embassy made a strong complaint.'

'Why did you do that? Aren't you allies?'

He looked at me sideways and smiled mockingly. 'No one is more fond than I of our Teutonic brothers (for you know

the Germans let our people think they are Mohammedans).
According to the German idea, perhaps, the taking of Warsaw
was also a Turkish victory. But we are getting touchy about
the spread of German flags in the city.'

I noticed that many shops and hotels had signs newly
painted in French, but that on most of them the European
languages had been eliminated.

'You will be amused by that,' said Daoud Bey. 'You see,
when the war broke out, the government issued an order that
no one in Turkey should use the language of a hostile nation.
The French newspapers were suppressed, the French and
English signs ordered removed; people were forbidden to
speak French, English, or Russian; and letters written in the
three languages were simply burned. But they soon found out
that the greater part of the population on this side of the
Golden Horn speak only French, and no Turkish at all; so
they had to let up. As for letters, that was simple. The American consul protested; so just a week ago the papers printed
a solemn order of the government that, although French,
English, and Russian were still barred, you might write letters
in American!'

Daoud Bey was a Turk of wealthy, prominent family –
which is extraordinary in Turkey, where families rise and fall
in one generation, and there is no family tradition because
there is no family name. Daoud, son of Hamid, was all we
knew him by; just as I, to the Turkish police, was known as
John, son of Charles. In that splendid idle way Turks have,
Daoud had been made an admiral in the navy at the age of
nineteen. Some years later a British naval commission, by
invitation, reorganized the Turkish fleet. Now, it is difficult to
pry wealthy young Turks loose from their jobs. The commission therefore asked Daoud Bey very politely if he would
like to continue being an admiral. He answered: 'I should like
to very much, provided I never have to set foot on a ship. I
can't bear the sea.' So he is no longer in the navy.

I asked him why he was not bleeding and dying with his compatriots in the trenches at Gallipoli.

'Of course,' said he, 'you Westerners cannot be expected to understand. Here you buy out of military service by paying forty liras. If you don't buy out it amounts to the admission that you haven't forty liras – which is very humiliating. No Turk of any prominence could afford to be seen in the army, unless, of course, he entered the upper official grades as a career. Why, my dear fellow, if I were to serve in this war the disgrace would kill my father. It is quite different from your country. Here the recruiting sergeants beg you to pay your exemption fee – and they jeer at you if you haven't got it!'

At the foot of the hill there is a tangle of meeting streets – Step Street, that used to be the only way to clamber up to Pera; the wriggling narrow alleys that squirm through a Greek quarter of tall, dirty houses to infamous Five-Piastre and Ten-Piastre Streets in the vicious sailor town of Galata; the one street that leads to the cable tunnel, where the cars climb underground to the top of the hill – all opening into the square of Kara-keuy before the *Valideh Sultan Keuprisi*, the far-famed Outer Bridge that leads to Stamboul. White-frocked toll-collectors stood there in rippling rank, closing and parting before the throng, to the rattling chink of ten-para pieces falling into their outstretched hands. And flowing between them like an unending torrent between swaying piles, poured that bubbling ferment of all races and all religions – from Pera to Stamboul, and from Stamboul to Pera. Floating silk Arab head-dresses, helmets, turbans of yellow and red, smart fezzes, fezzes with green turbans around them to mark the relative of the Prophet, fezzes with white turbans around them – priests and teachers – Persian *tarbouches*, French hats, panamas. Veiled women in whose faces no man looked, hurrying along in little groups, robed in *tcharchafs* of black and grey and light brown, wearing extravagantly high-heeled French slippers too big for their feet, and followed by an old black female slave; Arabs from the Syrian desert in floating white cloaks; a saint from the country, bearded to the eyes, with squares of flesh showing through his coloured rags, striding along, muttering prayers, with turban all awry, while a little crowd of disciples pressed after to kiss his hand and whine a blessing; bare-legged Armenian porters staggering at a smooth trot, bent under great packing-cases and shouting '*Destour!*' to clear the way; four soldiers on foot with new rifles; helmeted police on horseback; shambling eunuchs in frock coats; a Bulgarian bishop; three Albanians in blue broadcloth trousers and jackets embroidered with silver; two Catholic Sisters of Charity walking at the head of their little donkey-cart, presented to them by the Mohammedan merchants of the Great Bazaar; a *mevlevi*, or dancing dervish, in tall conical felt hat and grey robes; a bunch of German tourists in Tyrolean hats, equipped with open Baedekers, and led by a plausible Armenian guide; and representatives of five hundred fragments of strange races, left behind by the great invasions of antiquity in the holes and corners of Asia Minor. Pera is European – Greek, Armenian, Italian – anything but Turkish. Where goes this exotic crowd that pours into Pera? You never see them there.

A thousand venders of the most extraordinary merchandise – Angora honey, *helva, loukoum* of roses, *kaymak* (made from the milk of buffaloes shut in a dark stable), obscene postal cards, cigarette-holders of German glass, Adrianople melons, safety-pins, carpets manufactured in Newark, New Jersey, celluloid beads – moved among the crowd shouting their wares, bellowing, whining, screaming: 'Only a cent, two cents – *On paras, bech paraya*.'

To the right lay the Port of Commerce, crowded with ships, and the Inner Bridge beyond, all up the splendid sweep of Golden Horn. Outside the bridge was a row of pontoons placed there to guard the port from English submarines, and against the barrier the *chirket hariés* – Bosphorus steamboats –

backing precipitously out with screaming whistles into the thick flock of *caïks* that scatter like a shoal of fish. Beyond, across the bright-blue dancing water, the coast of Asia rising faintly into mountains, with Scutari dotted white along the shore. Stamboul, plunging from that magnificent point, crowned with palaces and trees, into the sea.... From left to right the prodigious sweep of the city, and the great mosques: Agia Sophia, built by the Emperoror Justinian a thousand years ago, all clumsy great buttresses of faded red and yellow: the Mosque of Sultan Selim, who conquered Mecca; the Mosque of Sultan Achmet; Yeni Valideh Djami, at the end of the bridge; Sultan Suleyman the Magnificent – he who was a friend of François Premier; Sultan Bayazid....

The floating drawbridge swung slowly open with much confused shouting and the tugging of cables by sputtering launches to allow the passage of a German submarine coming up from the Dardanelles. She was awash, her conning-tower painted a vivid blue with white streaks – the colour most disguising in these bright seas; but a momentary cloud passed over the sun, and she stood out startling against the suddenly grey water.

'It takes them about an hour to close the bridge,' said Daoud Bey, and drew me into an alley between stone buildings, where little tables and stools hugged the shade of the wall, and a shabby old Turk in flapping slippers and a spotted fez served ices. Outside all roar and clamour, and hot sun beating on the pavement – here cool, quiet peace.

'Daoud Pasha!' said a laughing voice. It was a slender girl in a faded green *feridjé*, with bare brown feet, and a shawl pinned under her chin, in the manner of the very poor, who cannot afford a veil. She could not have been more than fifteen; her skin was golden, and her black eyes flashed mischievously.

'Eli!' cried Daoud, seizing her hand.

'Give me some money!' said Eli imperiously.

'I have no small money.'

'All right, then, give me big money.'

Daoud laughed and handed her a *medjidieh* – and she gave a scream of pleasure, clapped her hands, and was gone.

'Gypsy,' said Daoud, 'and the most beautiful girl in all Constantinople. Hamdi, a friend of mine, fell in love with her, and asked her into his harem. So she went to live at Eyoub. But two weeks later I came down here one day, and as I was taking my sherbet I heard a little voice at my elbow: "Daoud Pasha, some money please." It was Eli. She said she had tried to be a respectable married lady for fourteen days, because she really loved Hamdi. He was very kind to her – gave her clothes and jewels, and courted her like a lover. But she couldn't stand it any longer; begging on the streets was more fun – she loved the crowd so. So one night she let herself out of the harem door and swam across the Golden Horn!' He laughed and shrugged his shoulders: 'You can't tame a *chingani*.'

We paid. 'May God favour you!' the proprietor said gently, and a Turk sitting at our table bowed and mumbled: '*Afietolsoun!* May what you have eaten do you good!'

Outside on the wharf where the *caïks* were ranked, each boatman yelling as loud as he could, a blind old woman in rusty black crouched against the wall and held out her hand. Daoud dropped a copper in it. She raised her sightless eyes to us and said in a sweet voice: 'Depart smiling.'

'*Kach parava?* How much?' said Daoud. A deafening clamour of voices shouted indistinguishable things.

'Let us take the old man,' said my friend, pointing to a figure with a long white beard, burnt-orange skull-cap, red sash, and pink shirt open at the throat to show his hairy old chest. 'How much, *effendim?*' he used the term of respect which all Turks use toward each other, no matter what the difference in their ranks.

'Five piastres,' said the old man hopefully.

'I pay one piastre and a half,' answered Daoud, climbing into the *caïk*. Without reply the *caïkji* pushed off.

'What is your name, my father?' asked Daoud.

'My name is Abdul, my son,' said the old man, rowing and sweating in the sun. 'I am born of Mohammed the Short-legged in the city of Trebizond on the sea. For fifty-two years I have been rowing my *caïk* across the Stamboul Limani.'

I told Daoud to ask him what he thought of the war.

'It is a good war,' said Abdul. 'All wars against the *giaour* are good, for does not the Koran say that he who dies slaying the infidel will enter paradise?'

'You are learned in the Koran?' exclaimed Daoud. 'Perhaps, you are a *sheikh* and lead prayers in the mosque.'

'Do I wear the white turban?' said the old man. 'I am no priest; but in my youth I was a *muezzin*, and called to prayers from the minaret.'

'What should he know of the war?' I said. 'It doesn't touch him personally.'

Daoud translated.

'I have four sons and two grandsons in the war,' said Abdul, with dignity. Then to me: 'Are you an *Aleman* – a German – one of our brothers who do not know our language and do not wear the fez? Tell me, of what shape and build are your mosques? Is your Sultan as great as our Sultan?'

I replied evasively that he was very great.

'We shall win this war, *inshallah* – God willing,' said Abdul.

'*Mashallah!*' responded Daoud gravely, and I saw that his light European cynicism was a thin veneer over eight centuries of deep religious belief.

Seventeen

THE HEART OF STAMBOUL

Our *caïk* ran into a thick tangle of *caïks* clamorous with shouting, arguing boatmen, Abdul standing upright and screaming: *Verdah!* Make way, sons of animals! Make way for the passengers! You have no passengers, why do you block the landing-place?' We laid our piastre and a half on the thwart and leaped ashore in Stamboul. Through the narrow, winding street piled high with melons and vegetables and water-casks, and overhung by ragged awnings propped on sticks, we jostled an amazing crowd of porters, *mullahs*, merchants, pilgrims, and peddlers. In the Oriental way, no one moved from our road – we bumped along.

Along a cross street a string of boys and young men – each one carrying a loaf of bread – marched by between double lines of soldiers.

'Recruits,' said Daoud Bey. Often we met a non-commissioned officer and two armed men prowling among the crowds, glancing sharply in the faces of the young men; they were looking for possible soldiers who had not yet been called. Shouts and the trampling of feet, angry bellows and screams of pain drew our attention to a side alley, where a hundred men and women of all races swirled against the front of a shop; fez tassels danced in the air, grasping hands leaped out and sank, choking voices yelled, and on the outskirts two policemen beat any back they could reach – thwack! thwack! 'Waiting to buy bread,' explained Daoud. 'Hundreds of places like that all over Constantinople. There's plenty of grain in Anatolia, but the army needs the freight-cars – so they say.'

I said it ought to be an easy matter to feed the city.

'Possibly,' he answered with ironical inflection. 'Have you heard the rumour that the city officials are holding back the supply so as to get higher prices? Base falsehood, of course – yet such things have happened before. And then our German brothers are more or less responsible. They persuaded our government to take a census of the city – a thing which has never before been possible since the fifteenth century. But trust the Germans to find a way. The government took over the bakeries and closed them for three days, while it was announced that every one must apply for a bread-ticket in order to buy bread. By slow degrees they are getting us all registered – for a man must eat. Last evening, in the back streets of Pera, I came upon a bakery where the last load had just been distributed, with a howling mob outside still unprovided for. First they smashed the windows, in spite of the clubbing of the police, and then they began to tear down the Turkish flags hung out on all the houses to celebrate the fall of Novo-Georgievsk, crying: "We don't care for victories! Give us bread!" '

We sat cross-legged in the booth of Youssof Effendi the Hoja, in the *Misr Tcharshee*, or Bazaar of Egypt, where drugs are sold. Dim light filtered through cobweb windows high up in the arched roof that covered in the bazaar – making a cool gloom rich with the smells of perfumes, drugs, herbs, and strange Oriental medicines, of coffee from Aden, of tea from southern Persia. Overhead the whitewashed arch was scrawled with immense black whorls and loops of prayers to Allah, and Esculapian snakes twisted into verses out of the Koran. Above the booth was an intricate cornice of carved wood, covered with spider-webs, and from this vague twilight depended all sorts of strange objects on chains: dervish beggar-bowls made from the brittle skin of sea animals, ostrich eggs, tortoise-shells, two human skulls, and what was evidently the lower jaw of a horse. On the counter and the shelves behind were crowded glass bottles and earthen pots full of crude amber, lumps of camphor, hashish in powder and in the block, Indian and Chinese opium and the weak opium of Anatolia, bunches of dried herbs to cure the plague, black powder for love philters, crystals of oil for aphrodisiacs, charms to avert the evil eye and to confound your enemies, attar of roses, blocks of sandalwood, and sandal oil. In the dark little room behind the shop were heaped bales and jars, so that when Youssof Effendi lighted his lamp it looked and smelled like the cave of the Forty Thieves.

He stopped us, bowing with the right hand sweeping down, and fluttering to lips and forehead again and again; a tall, dignified figure in a long caftan of grey silk, and fez with the white turban of a religious teacher wound about it – immaculate. A glossy black beard covered his powerful mouth and dazzling teeth, and he had dark, shrewd, kindly eyes.

'*Salaam aleykoum*, Daoud Bey,' said he softly. 'Peace be with you.'

'*Aleykoum salaam*, Youssof Effendi,' answered Daoud, rapidly making the gesture and touching lips and forehead. 'Here is my friend from America.'

'*Hosh geldin*. You are welcome,' said the Hoja courteously to me, with a constant motion of his hands to lips and forehead. He didn't say '*salaam*,' which is only used between Mohammedans. The Hoja knew only Turkish.

'Bedri!' he cried and clapped his hands, and a little boy scurried out from somewhere in the bowels of the shop. 'Coffee, *haide*!...'

We sat sipping the sweet thick liquid, smoking in long wooden *chibouks* cigarettes that we rolled of choice tobacco from Samsoun, in the cool, fragrant gloom.

'Is the *effendim* well?' murmured the Hoja gently, in the

ritual of Oriental politeness; each sip we took, each puff at our cigarettes he touched his lips and forehead, and we to him. 'May God make it pleasant to your stomachs.'

The Hoja was a powerful man in Stamboul. For twenty years he had been *muezzin* in the mosque of Zeirick Kilissi, which was once the church of St Saviour Pantocrator, and in whose shadow still lies the *verde antique* sarcophagus of the Empress Irene; then a leader of prayers on Friday in the great mosques; a popular teacher and charm doctor; and finally sent for by Abdul Hamid to lead private prayers in Yildiz Kiosk, those long years the Sultan shut himself up there in fear of assassination.

'I know many fables about the marvels of America,' said Youssof Effendi graciously. 'There appear to be palaces taller than those raised by the *djinni* in ancient times, and I have heard there is a demon called Graft' – here his eyes twinkled – 'who stalks through your streets and devours people, and is known in no other land. One day I shall go there, for I understand that there opium is worth its weight in gold.'

He looked from Daoud Bey to me. 'You are different from us, you races of the West,' he remarked. 'Daoud Bey is handsome, but he is over-refined and thinks too much. He will have nervous jumps some day. He should not smoke tobacco, but eat plenty of eggs and milk. Tell the American *effendi* that I think he does not think too much and is very happy. That is the way I am.'

I wanted Daoud to ask how many wives he had. The Hoja understood my ill-mannered curiosity and smiled.

'*Pekki!* How many wives has the effendi?' he replied. 'Does he think that it is any easier for a Mohammedan to support two wives than a Christian? Allah preserve us! Women are expensive. I know but six friends who have more than one wife. When the Armenian slave dealers come by night to my harem from Scutari with a fair *odalik* to sell, I answer them with a proverb: "How many bodies can live of one man's meat?" '

'What does Youssof Effendi think of the war?'

'The war?' he answered, and the evasive look on his face showed that I had touched on a subject in which he was deeply involved. 'My son is in the trenches at Gallipoli. Allah send what he will! One does not think of whether wars are good or bad. We are a fighting race, we Osmanlis.'

'Do the Turks –' I began.

The Hoja interrupted me with a sputtering torrent of language.

'You must not call us "Turks," ' said Daoud. ' "Turk" means rustic clown – "rude," as you would say. We are not Turcomans, barbaric, bloodthirsty savages from Central Asia; we are Osmanlis, an ancient and civilized race.'

The Hoja talked frankly of the Germans. 'I do not like them,' he said. 'They have no manners. When an Englishman or an American has been one month in Turkey, he comes to my booth with hand to lips, to forehead, and greets me: "*Sabah sherifiniz hair ola.*" Before he buys, he accepts my coffee and my cigarettes, and we talk of indifferent subjects, as is proper. But when the Germans come they salute as they do in their army, and refuse my coffee, and want to buy and be gone, without friendship. I do not sell any more to *Alemanes*.'

Later I observed many of the Germans around the city; there were hundreds of them – officers on leave, tourists, and civil officials. Often they violated the delicate etiquette that governs Mohammedan life. They spoke to veiled women on the street; bullied merchants in the Great Bazaar; stamped noisily into mosques during the hour of prayer on Friday, when no European is allowed to enter, and once at a *tekkeh* of the Howling Dervishes I was present in the visitors' gallery, while two German officers read aloud passages from the

Koran in German throughout the services – to the furious indignation of the priests. . . .

We went up with Youssof Effendi through the intricate winding streets of Stamboul, plunging into passages lined with tiny Armenian shops, under the walls of the fortress-like *khans* built for the entertainment of strangers by the mothers of bygone Sultans, by secret paths across the quiet courtyards of the great mosques, where children played about delicately carved marble fountains in the shade of enormous ancient trees; down little streets that twisted beneath the wooden booths of the seal-makers and sellers of *tesbiehs* – bead-chains – where green vines fell like cascades from the roofs; into vast sun-smitten dusty squares, the site of Byzantine forums and of coliseums greater than Rome's; through winding alleys of wooden houses with overhanging *shah-nichars*, where there was only an occasional passer-by – a shrill-voiced peddler beating his donkey, a grave-faced *imam*, women hurrying along with averted faces.

When we passed women Daoud began to talk German in a loud voice.

'They think you are a German officer,' he said, laughing, 'and it makes a terrible hit. All the harems are learning German now, and a lieutenant from Berlin or Hanover is the romantic ideal of most Turkish women!'

Half the people we met saluted the Hoja – saluted him humbly as a person of prominence and power. In the unending maze of covered streets which makes up the Great Bazaar, a double chorus of cries came from both sides: 'Youssof Effendi, buy of me! See this beautiful *chibouk*! Honour me with your patronage, Youssof Effendi!' In the Bechistan, that gloomy great square where are the jewels and precious metals, the gold-and-silver-inlaid weapons and ancient carpets we moved from counter to counter in triumph, followed by the *sheikh* of the Bechistan himself.

'What is the price of this?' asked the Hoja imperiously.

'A Turkish pound, *effendim*.'

'Robber and thief,' replied our guide calmly. 'I will give you five piastres.' He moved on, flinging back over his shoulder: 'Dog of a Jew, we go and return no more!'

'Ten piastres! Ten piastres!' screamed the man, while the *sheikh* berated him for his discourtesy to the great Youssof Effendi....

For me he beat down a nervous shouting salesman on an amber *chibouk*, from two and a half pounds to twenty piastres.

'Do not make me shout, Youssof Effendi!' he yelled, his voice breaking, and the sweat standing out on his brow. 'You will give me apoplexy!'

'Twenty piastres,' said the Hoja calmly, inexorably.

Late in the morning we sat in the dark cubbyhole behind a little Greek bookshop near the Sublime Porte, looking at hand-illuminated Korans – Daoud Bey, myself, and the clever, pleasant proprietor. Enter a young policeman, in grey coat with red epaulets and a fez of grey astrakhan. He came to where we sat, sighed deeply, and began in a melancholy voice a long story in Turkish. Daoud translated.

'I have eaten offal,' said the policeman. 'I have been greatly humiliated. Several days ago I observed Ferid Bey and Mahmoud Bey sitting in a café talking to an unveiled girl of the streets, who was a Greek. Ferid Bey came to me and said: "You must arrest Mahmoud Bey." "Why for?" I asked. "Because he is talking piggishness to a girl." I was very much surprised. "I did not know that talking piggishness to a girl was against the law," I said. "I am a friend of Bedri Bey, the chief of police," said Ferid Bey, "and I demand that you arrest Mahmoud Bey for talking piggishness to that girl." So I arrested Mahmoud Bey and took him to jail.

'He was in prison for three days, because everybody had

forgotten all about him; but at last the keeper of the jail telephoned Bedri Bey, and asked what to do with Mahmoud Bey. Bedri Bey replied that he knew nothing of the man or the matter, so why keep him in prison? Therefore, they let Mahmoud Bey loose, and he telephoned at once to Bedri Bey, and made a complaint about being arrested, "Talking piggishness," said he, "is no offence against the law." Then Bedri Bey called me before him and applied epithets to me, like "son of an animal," and threatened to dismiss me. Together Mahmoud Bey and I went to arrest Ferid Bey. But he was gone, he and the girl together. Then Mahmoud Bey boxed my ears. I am humiliated. I have eaten offal.'

We dined in the restaurant of the Municipal Garden of the Petit Champs at Pera, to the blaring rag-time of the band. The striped awning over the terrace was gay in a flood of yellow light, and electric-lamps hanging high in the full-leaved trees made a dim, chequered shade on the people sitting drinking at iron tables, and the cosmopolitan parade that moved round and round the garden. Vague under the smoky radiance of an immense yellow moon, the Golden Horn glittered, speckled with the red and green lights of ships; beyond lay the dim, obscure mass of Stamboul, like a crouching animal.

The diners were mostly Germans and Austrians – officers on leave, aide-de-camps on duty at the Seraskierat in full-dress Turkish uniform, civilian officials, and the highly paid workmen of the Krupp factories; many of them with wives and children, in comfortable bourgeois dinner-parties like the restaurants of Berlin. But there were also Frenchmen with smartly dressed wives, English, Italians, and Americans. In the slowly moving throng outside under the trees, were Perote Greeks, Armenians, Levantine Italians, Turks of official rank; German submarine sailors, Germans of the Turkish navy in fezzes, and great rolling ruddy American sailors from the stationnaire *Scorpion*, towering in their white summer uniform head and shoulders above the crowd. It was hard to believe that, just beyond the reach of our ears, the great guns spat and boomed unceasingly day and night across the bitter sands of Gallipoli. . . .

If I had only space to recount the Homeric battles of those American sailors! The German man-of-war's-men and soldiers were friendly, but the workmen and civilians very quarrelsome. Sometimes an intoxicated or excited Teuton would come over to the American table and begin an argument about munitions of war, or the *Lusitania* case; or a German officer in Turkish uniform would stop them on the street and insist on being saluted. The sailors answered nothing but insults, and then they answered with their fists, Anglo-Saxon fashion. I could write another chapter simply about the night that Seaman Williams broke the German lieutenant's head with a stone beer-mug, and was transferred back to the United States as being 'unfit for diplomatic service.' And then there is the wonderful history of the two sailors who laid out seventeen attacking Germans in a café, and were led back to the American Sailors' Club by congratulatory police, while the wounded foe were jailed for three days. . . . Respect and friendship was mutual between the American sailors and the Turkish police. . . .

Afterward we got into a cab and drove down the steep, dark streets to the Inner Bridge; the cabman carefully shrouded his lamps, for lights on the bridges were forbidden on account of possible lurking British submarines. Stamboul was black – they were saving coal. Dim lamps in the interiors of little stores and cafés shed a flickering illumination on mysterious figures shrouded in the voluminous garments of the East, who drifted silently by on slippered feet.

Youssof Effendi was in his favourite café in a street behind the Bayazid mosque. We sat there with him, talking and drinking coffee, and puffing lazily at our *narghilehs* – the grey, cool smoke that makes the sweat stand out on your forehead. ... Later we walked through the darkness across the city, by ways known to him alone, through arched passages, broken walls, and mosque courtyards. One after the other on mighty minarets, the *muezzins* came out into the heavy night, and cried that quavering singsong which carries so far, and seems the last requiem of an old religion and a worn-out race.

Out of his great courtesy, the Hoja insisted on going with us to Pera; so we invited him to drink a coffee with us at the Petit Champs. On the open-air stage the regular evening vaudeville performance was going on – singing girls, dancing girls, American tramp comedian, Hungarian acrobats, German marionettes – the harsh voices, lascivious gestures, suggestive costumes, ungraceful writhings of the Occident. How vulgar it seemed after the dignified quiet of Stamboul, the exquisite courtesy of Turkish life!

Some Turkish officers from the interior of Asia Minor, who had never before seen women publicly unveiled and showing their legs, sat gaping in the front row, alternately flushing with anger and shame and roaring with laughter at the amazing indecency of the civilized West. ... The Hoja watched the performance attentively, but his polished politeness gave no sign of embarrassment. Soon it ended, and in spite of many protests on the Hoja's part, we walked down the hill to the bridge with him. He did not speak of the show at all. But I was curious to know his real opinion.

'It was very lovely,' replied Youssof Effendi with the most suave courtesy: 'I shall take my little granddaughter to see it. ...'

Down at the dark bridge the draw was open, to let pass a contraband ship full of coal and oil which had crept down the coast from Burgas. Now at night it is forbidden for all but high officers to cross the Golden Horn in *caïks*, so there seemed nothing to do but wait for the interminable closing of the draw. Daoud Bey, however, confidently led the way down to the landing-place. Suddenly, out of the shadow popped a soldier-patrol.

'*Dour!* Stop!' cried the officer. 'Where are you going?'

Daoud turned on him rudely. '*Wir sind Deutsche offizieren!*' he bellowed. The man saluted hastily, and fell back into the dark. 'The German always does it,' chuckled Daoud....

Late at night we climbed once more up Pera Hill. In a dark side-street the crowd was already beginning to gather about the front of a bakery, to stand there until it opened in the morning. We were stopped at Tramway Street by a flock of tooting automobiles rushing up, and street-cars one after another with clanging bells. Through the dark windows we glimpsed white faces staring out, bandaged – another Red Crescent ship had arrived from the front, and they were hurrying the wounded to the hospitals.

Eighteen

RUMANIA IN DIFFICULTIES

My window, high up in the dazzling neo-French façade of the Athenée Palace Hotel in Bucharest, looks down on a little park smothered in almost tropical luxuriance of trees and flowers, where busts of minor Rumanian celebrities on marble columns stonily ignore each his marble wreath proffered by the languishing Muse kneeling on the pedestal. You've seen millions like them all over France. To the left lies the *Atheneul*, combining the functions of the Louvre, the Pantheon, and the Trocadero, and built to suggest the architecture of the Paris Opera. Its baroque dome bears aloft a frieze of gilt lyres, and the names of the great dead in gilt letters: Shakespeare, Cervantes, Pushkin, Camoens, Beethoven, Racine, etc., and two or three Rumanians unknown to the West. Eastward as far as one can see, red-tile roofs and white-stone copings pile up, broken with vivid masses of trees – palaces and mansions and hotels of the most florid modern French style, with an occasional Oriental dome or the bulb of a Rumanian Greek Church. It is like a pleasure city built by Frenchmen in the south, this little 'Paris of the Balkans,' whose Rumanian name, *Bucureshti*, means literally 'City of Joy.'

At sunset the town wakes from the baking heat of a cloud-less summer day. On the right the principal and smartest street, Calea Victoriei, winds roaring between the High-Life Hotel (pronounced 'Hig-Liff') and the Jockey Club building – which might have been bodily transplanted from the Boulevard Haussmann. All the world is driving home from the races down on the Chaussée – a combination of the Bois de Boulogne and the Champs Elysées – where it has seen the stable of Mr Alexandre Marghiloman, chief of the Germanophile branch of the Conservative party, win the Derby as usual – one, two, three. The regular evening parade begins. An endless file of handsome carriages, drawn by superb pairs of horses, trots smartly by in both directions along the twisting, narrow street. The coachmen wear blue-velvet robes to their feet, belted with bright satin ribbons whose ends flutter out behind, so you can guide them right or left by pulling the proper tab. These are public cabs owned communally by their drivers, who are all members of a strange Russian religious sect expelled from their own country; their belief requires that after they have married and had one child, they shall become eunuchs. . . .

Each carriage is the setting for a woman or two women, rouged, enamelled, and dressed more fantastically than the wildest poster girl imagined by French decorators. A dense crowd overflowing from the sidewalks into the street moves slowly from the *Atheneul* up past the King's palace to the boulevards and back again – extravagant women, and youths made up like French decadent poets, and army officers in uniforms of pastel shades, with much gold lace, tassels on their boots, and caps of baby-blue and salmon-pink – colour combinations that would make a comic-opera manager sick with envy. They have puffy cheeks and rings under their eyes, these officers, and their cheeks are sometimes painted, and they spend all their time riding up and down the Calea with their mistresses, or eating cream puffs at Capsha's pastryshop, where all prominent and would-be prominent Bucharestians show themselves every day, and where the vital affairs of the nation are settled. What a contrast between the officers and the rank and file of the army – strong, stocky little peasants who swing by in squads to the blare of bugles, excellently equipped and trained! The numberless cafés and pastry-shops spill tables out on the sidewalk and the streets, crowded with debauched-looking men and women got up like chorus-girls. In the open café-gardens the gypsy orchestras swing into wild rhythms that get to be a habit like strong drink; a hundred restaurants fill with exotic crowds. Lights flash out. Shop windows gleam with jewels and costly things that men buy for their mistresses. Ten thousand public women parade – for your true Bucharestian boasts that his city supports more prostitutes in proportion than any other four cities in the world combined....

To look at it all you would imagine that Bucharest was as ancient as Sofia or Belgrade. The white stone weathers so swiftly under the hot, dry sun, the oily rich soil bears such a mellowing abundance of vegetation, life is so complex and sophisticated – yet thirty years ago there was nothing here but a wretched village, some old churches, and an older monastery which was the seat of a princely family. Bucharest is a get-rich city, and modern Rumanian civilization is like that – a mushroom growth of thirty years. The fat plain is one of the greatest grain-growing regions in the world, and there are mountains covered with fine timber; but the mainspring of wealth is the oil region. There are oil kings and timber kings and land kings, quickly and fabulously wealthy. It costs more to live in Bucharest than in New York.

There is nothing original about the city, nothing individual. Everything is borrowed. A dinky little German King lives in a dinky little palace that looks like a French Prefecture, surrounded by a pompous little court. The government is modelled on that of Belgium. Although all titles of nobility except in the King's immediate family were abolished years ago, many people call themselves 'Prince' and 'Count' because their forefathers were Moldavian and Wallachian *boyars*; not to speak of the families who trace their descent from the Emperors of Byzantium! Poets and artists and musicians and

doctors and lawyers and politicians have all studied in Paris –
and of late Vienna, Berlin, or Munich. Cubism is more cubic
and futurism more futuristic in Rumania than at home. Fren-
chified little policemen bully the market-bound peasants, who
dare to drive across the Calea Victoriei and interrupt the
procession of kept women. Cabarets and music-halls are like
the less amusing places on Montmartre; you can see Revues
based on dull French ones, copies of risqué comedies straight
from the Théâtre Antoine, or the National Theatre – which
imitates the Comédie Française, and looks like the Municipal
Theatre at Lyons. A surface coating of French frivolity covers
everything – without meaning and without charm.

If you want to infuriate a Rumanian, you need only speak
of his country as a Balkan state.

'Balkan!' he cries. 'Balkan! Rumania is not a Balkan state.
How dare you confuse us with half-savage Greeks or Slavs!
We are *Latins*.'

One is never allowed to forget that; the newspapers insist
every day that Rumanians are Latins – every day there is a
reference to 'our brothers, the French, or the Spaniards, or
the Italians' – but really of purer blood than these 'brothers,'
for the Rumanians are descendants of Roman veterans colon-
ized in Transylvania by the Emperor Trajan. Some local
writers complacently insist that Rumania is the inheritor of
the Roman Empire; in a square in Bucharest there is a fountain
showing Romulus and Remus suckled by the wolf, and some
of the public buildings are adorned with the Insignia, the
Fasces, the Eagle, and 'S. P. Q. R.' But those Roman colonists
may have been originally drafted into the legions from Tarsus,
or the suburbs of Jerusalem or south Germany. Add to that
the blood of the native Dacians, a strong Slavic strain, Magyar,
Vlaque, and a great deal of gypsy, and you have the Rumanian.... He speaks a Latin language strongly impregnated with
Slavic and Asiatic roots – an inflexible tongue to use, and
harsh and unmusical to the ear. And he has Latin traits:

excitability, candour, wit, and a talent for hysterical argument in critical situations. He is lazy and proud, like a Spaniard, but without a Spaniard's flavour; sceptical and libertine, like a Frenchman, but without a Frenchman's taste; melodramatic and emotional, like an Italian, without Italian charm. One good observer has called Rumanians 'bad Frenchmen,' and another 'Italianized gypsies.' Shopkeepers and cabmen and waiters in restaurants are thieving and ungracious; if they can't cheat you they fly into a ugly rage and scream like angry monkeys. How many times have Rumanian friends said to me: 'Don't go to so-and-so's shop; he is a Rumanian and will cheat you. Find a German or French place.'

It will be said that I have judged Rumanians by the people of Bucharest, and that Bucharest is not all Rumania. But I insist that the metropolis reflects the dominant traits of any nation – that Paris is essentially French, Berlin essentially Prussian, and Bucharest thoroughly Rumanian. Sometimes there are peasants on the street; the men in white linen trousers, and shirts that fall to their knees, embroidered in delicate designs of flowers, the women in richly decorated linen skirts and blouses of drawn work exquisitely worked in colour, chains of gold coins hanging around their necks. They fit into the comic-opera scheme of things. But one hour by automobile from Bucharest you come upon a village where the people live in burrows in the ground, covered with roofs of dirt and straw. The ground their burrows are dug in is owned by a *boyar* – a landowning noble – who keeps a racing stable in France, and they till his land for him. Two per cent of the population can read and write. There is no school there. Several years ago the proprietor himself built a school for his people, on condition that the government would take it over and support it; for three years now it has been used as a storehouse.

These peasants eat nothing but corn – not because they are vegetarians but because they are too poor to eat meat. And

146

the church provides frequent fasts, which are the subject of laudatory comments on 'frugality and thrift' by satisfied landowners. The peasants are very religious, or superstitious, whichever you want to call it. For instance, they believe that if a man dies without a lighted candle in his hand to guide him through the dark corridors of death, he will not reach heaven. Now many people *do* die suddenly without the lighted candle; and here is where the church comes in. The country priest charges the dead man's family eighty francs to get him into heaven without the candle, and a certain sum yearly to keep him there. The priest also takes advantage of the vampire legend – a superstition, widely believed in Hungary, the Balkans, and South Russia. If a peasant dies and others from his family or village follow in quick succession, the priest suggests that the dead man's spirit is a vampire. To lay this murdering ghost, the body must be exhumed in the dead of night (for it is strictly forbidden by Rumanian criminal law) and the heart torn out by an ordained priest, who drives a wooden peg through it. For this he charges a hundred francs.

Once I went north on a night train which carried the Crown Prince's private car. It was a cold night, with a wind that ate into your bones. Yet all night long we looked from our window upon a line of wretched peasants standing beside the track, one every quarter of a mile, ragged and shivering, holding torches above their heads to do honour to their prince....

Never was a country so ripe for revolution. More than fifty per cent of the arable land is owned by less than ten per cent of the country's landowners – some four and a half thousand big proprietors out of a population of seven and a half millions, seven-eighths of whom are working peasants; and this in spite of the fact that the government has been breaking up the big estates and selling land to the people since 1864. The *boyars* and great landholders seldom live on their estates. Indeed, it is all they can do to keep up their hotels in Paris and Vienna, their houses in Bucharest, their villas at Nice, Constantza, and Sinaia, their winters on the Riviera, art galleries, racing stables, and general blowing of money in the four quarters of the world. One family I met posed as great humanitarians because they provided mud huts for their people, and paid them twenty cents a day – with the cost of living almost what it is in New Jersey. Add to this hopeless condition of affairs the fact that all voters in Rumania are divided into three classes, on the basis of their incomes, so that about one hundred peasants' votes equal one rich man's vote. There have been several revolutions in Rumania, the last one purely agrarian, in 1907; but since the conscript army system exists, it is easy to order peasants in the south to shoot down their northern brothers, and vice versa. You have only to see the Rumanian peasants, gentle, submissive, with almost effeminate dress, manners – even their national songs and dances are pretty and soft – to realize how frightful the pressure that would force them to revolt.

What is the trend of Rumanian public opinion? There is no public opinion in Rumania. The peasants will fight for whatever their masters decide will give them the greatest country to exploit. It is simply another demonstration of how military service delivers a nation bound hand and foot to ambitious politicians. So one must ask the politicians, and they will reply that Rumania will join the side that satisfies 'national aspirations' – as they call cupidity in the Balkans.

Now the Rumanians came originally from Translyvania, and settled the flat plain north of the Danube which includes Bessarabia, and stretches eastward to the Black Sea. A race of herders and farmers, they spread far; southern Bucovina is full of Rumanians, and they are found in compact groups throughout Bulgaria, Serbia, the Banat, Macedonia, and Greece. The most civilized section, Transylvania, was early drawn into the Hungarian kingdom; Bucovina was a present

from the Turkish Sultan to the Emperor Joseph, and Bessarabia, twice Rumanian, was finally taken by Russia as the
price of Rumanian independence after the battle of Plevna.
And although many people now alive remember the passing
of the Russian armies that freed Rumania from the Turk, they
cannot forget the two million Rumanians who fell under the
Russian yoke. It was partially to make up for the loss of that
great province that Rumania stabbed Bulgaria in the back in
1913, and took away Silistria, where there was no Rumanian
population. When there is no other reason for territorial
conquest, this kind of 'national aspirations' is excused by
Balkanians on 'strategical grounds.'

Bessarabia was forcibly Russianized. The upper classes, of
course, easily became Russian, but the prohibition of the
Rumanian language in schools and churches had the effect of
driving the peasants out of both – of making a brutalized
and degraded race, who have lost all connection with or
knowledge of their mother country.

In Transylvania, the birthplace of the race, and the Banat
beyond, there are some three million Rumanians. But there,
in spite of the desperate Hungarian campaign to Magyarize
the people as the Russians did in Bessarabia, the racial feeling
is strong and growing. The Transylvanians are rich and civilized; when the Rumanian tongue was banned in the higher
schools and the churches, they fought a stubborn fight, crossing the mountains into Rumania for education, and spreading
the nationalist propaganda at home and abroad so thoroughly
that every Rumanian knows and feels for his oppressed brothers on the other side of the Carpathians, and you can travel
across Hungary as far as Buda-Pesth and beyond without
speaking any language but Rumanian.

So the 'national aspirations' of Rumania, on 'eth-
nographical grounds,' include Bessarabia, Bucovina, Transylvania, and the Banat; and I have also seen a map in
Bucharest, coloured to show that Macedonia should really

belong to Rumania, because *the majority of the population are Rumanians!*

All this does not excite the peasant to the verge of war on any side. But there is a mortal wrestling-match going on between pro-Teuton and pro-Ally politicians. How many obscure lawyers are now getting rich in the limelight of political prominence! In the Balkans politics is largely a personal matter; newspapers are the organs of individual men who have jockeyed themselves to be party leaders, in countries where a new party is born every hour over a glass of beer in the nearest café. For instance, *La Politique* is the organ of the millionaire Marghiloman, lately chief of the Conservative party and only partially deposed. He was once so pro-French that it is said he used to send his laundry to Paris – but the Germans got him. His pro-Ally constituents split off under Mr Filipescu, violently anti-German, whose organ is the *Journal des Balkans*. . . . Then there is the *Independence Roumaine*, property of the family of Mr Bratianu, the premier – who was pro-German at the beginning of the war, but has become mildly pro-Ally – chief of the Liberal party now in power. And *La Roumanie*, mouthpiece of Mr Take Ionescu, the leader of the Conservative Democrats, who is the most powerful force in the country on the side of the Entente Powers. The Conservatives are the great proprietors; the Liberals are the capitalists; the Conservative Democrats are about the same as our Progressives, and the peasants' Socialist Agrarian party doesn't count. But all internal programmes were forgotten at the question: On which side shall Rumania enter the war?

Two years ago old King Carol summoned a council of ministers and party leaders at Sinaia, and made a speech advocating immediate entrance on the side of the Central Powers. But when a vote was taken, only one man present was with the King. It was the first time his royal will had ever been thwarted, and a few days later he died without returning to the capital. Ferdinand, the present King, is in the same predicament, and, what is more, he has an English queen.... It is a great game being fought over the heads of the King and the people by powerful financial interests, and the ambitions of political jugglers.

Meanwhile, a steady stream of Russian gold has poured into willing pockets, and the methodical Teutons have been creating public sentiment in their own inimitable way. Thousands of Germans and Austrians descended upon Bucharest in holiday attire, their wallets bulging with money. The hotels were full of them. They took the best seats at every play, violently applauding things German and Rumanian, hissing things French and English. They printed pro-German newspapers and distributed them free to the peasants. Restaurants and gambling casinos, dear to the Rumanian heart, were bought by them. German goods at reduced prices flooded the shops. They supported all the girls, bought all the champagne, corrupted all the government functionaries they could reach.... A nationwide agitation was started about 'our poor oppressed brothers in Russian Bessarabia' – in order to divert attention from Transylvania and stir up anti-Russian feeling.

To the Rumanian Government, Germany and Austria offered Bessarabia, including even Odessa, and Bucovina would also be ceded if she insisted. The Allies offered Transylvania, the Banat, and the Bucovina plateau north of her frontier. Although there was much talk in the press about 'redeeming lost Bessarabia,' the Bessarabian question was really not a vital one, while the Transylvanian question was burning and immediate. Moreover, the Rumanians know that Russia is a coming nation, and that forty years from now, even if defeated in this war, she will be there just the same, and stronger; while Austria-Hungary is an old and disintegrating empire, whose drive will be no longer eastward.

Three times since the war began Rumania tentatively agreed with the Allies to enter – and three times she drew back: once in the early spring, when Russia was on the Carpathians, and again when Italy entered. The last time was when I saw Mr Take Ionescu at midnight of the day that Bulgaria signed her agreement with Turkey.

'I think Bulgaria has chosen her side,' he said very gravely. 'We are not such babies as to believe that Turkey would give up any territory for nothing. The Central Powers will drive through Serbia – only we can stop that. And I am in a position to tell you that Serbia can claim our help if she is attacked. The Austrians have closed their frontier to us, and four hundred thousand men are said to be massed ready to march on Bucharest. It is a bluff – a bluff to force the resignation of the Bratianu cabinet, and the calling of Mr Marghiloman to form a ministry – which would mean a German policy. Even if the Bratianu cabinet fell – which I doubt, for he is not for war – only he and the King working together could pave the way for Marghiloman. And that is impossible.'

Three weeks later the German drive on Serbia began; but once more Rumania held aloof.

Nineteen

BULGARIA GOES TO WAR

But the key to the Balkans is Bulgaria, not Rumania. Leaving Bucharest on a dirty little train, you crawl slowly south over the hot plain, passing wretched little villages made of mud and straw, like the habitations of an inferior tribe in Central Africa. Gentle, submissive-looking peasants in white linen, stand gaping stupidly at the engine. You stop at every tiny station, as if the Rumanian Government were contemptuously indifferent of any one going to Bulgaria, and at Giurgiu there is an unnecessarily rigid examination by petty despotic customs officials, who make it as disagreeable as possible to leave the country.

But across the yellow Danube is another world. While the steamer is yet a hundred yards from the landing-stage somebody hails you with a grin – a big brown policeman who has been in America, and whom you saw once as you passed that way two months ago. Good-natured, clumsy soldiers make a pretence of examining your baggage, and smile you a welcome. As you stand there a well-dressed stranger says in French: 'You are a foreigner, aren't you? Can I do anything for you?' He is not a guide; he is just a passenger like yourself, but a Bulgarian and therefore friendly. It is wonderful to see again the simple, flat, frank faces of mountaineers and free men, and to fill your ears with the crackling virility of Slavic speech. Bulgaria is the only country I know where you can speak to any one on the street and get a cordial answer –

where if a shopkeeper gives you the wrong change he will follow you to your hotel to return a two-cent piece. Never was sensation more poignant than our relief at being again in a real man's country.

The train labours up through Rustchuk – half Turkish with its minarets, spreading tile roofs, peasants wearing baggy trousers, red sashes, and turbans – into mighty uplands that roll south ever higher toward the mountains. A marriage procession passes; four ox-carts full of uproarious men and girls waving paper streamers, and gay with embroideries of white linen, chains of gold coins, bright-coloured blankets, bunches of grapes, and flowers. Ahead a man rides a mule, beating a drum, and a wild squadron of youths on horseback scurry shouting over the plain.... Night falls – the cold night of high altitudes – and you wake in the morning hurrying down a winding gorge beside a mountain torrent, between high hills of rocks and scrub, where herdsmen in brown homespun pasture their goats against the sky; past ravines in which little villages are caught, irregular and Turkish, their red roofs smothered in fruit-trees; until finally the mountains break, and you see Sofia crowning her little hill like a toy city of red and yellow, topped by her golden dome and over-shadowed by her mountain.

Nothing could be more different from Bucharest than Sofia. A sober little town of practical, ugly buildings, and clean streets paved with brick. Telephone-wires run overhead; many street-cars clang along. Except for an occasional ancient mosque or Byzantine ruin, and a sudden glimpse of shabby squares full of peasants in turbans squatting on their heels, it might be a bustling new city of the Pacific Northwest. There is one hotel where literally everybody goes – the Grand Hotel de Bulgaria; next door is the Grand Café de Bulgaria, where journalists make news, magnates plot and combine, lawyers blackmail, and politicians upset ministries. If you want an interview with the premier or one of the ministers – in one case I know of, with the King – you get a bell-boy of the Grand Hotel to call him up on the telephone. Of if you don't want to do that, simply take a table in the Grand Café – they will all come in some time during the day.... Sofia is a little place, friendly and accessible. The unpretentious Royal Palace is right across the street; the National Theatre one block down; the House of Parliament, or *Sobranié*, two blocks in the other direction, near the Foreign Office, and the Cathedral and Holy Synod just beyond. Every one of any importance lives in a radius of five blocks....

Toward evening the town gets on its best clothes, and strolls along the avenue of the Tsar Liberator to Prince Boris Park. It is a solemn domestic little parade of country people with their wives, daughters, sweethearts, and all the children. The women are comfortably unattractive, and they dress in last year's rural styles. Many officers mingle with the crowd – officers who wear smart, practical uniforms built for campaigning, and look as if they knew how to fight. Squads of burly soldiers in peaked caps and boots tramp stiffly by, roaring slow, hymn-like songs such as you hear in the Russian army....

Darkness brings a chill – for Sofia is a thousand feet up – and sharp on the stroke of eight the crowd scatters home to dinner. There is no restaurant except your hotel, and the food has no subtlety – ham and eggs and spinach being the Bulgarian's favourite dish. Afterward you can sit in the National Casino in the Public Gardens, and drink beer to the strains of a fine military band, or you can listen to interminable Bulgarian dialogues at the Municipal Theatre. There is only one music-hall, called 'New America,' a dreary place where heavily humorous comedians and unshapely dancers delight the guffawing peasants who have come to town on a jag.

The number of people who speak English is amazing. Almost all the political leaders have been educated at Roberts

College, the American missionary school in Constantinople. Roberts College has had such an influence on Bulgaria, that after the consolidation of the country and establishment of the kingdom in 1885, it was hailed as 'cradle of Bulgarian liberty.' That's why Sofia is so American, and that's why so many American methods are used in Bulgarian politics – even our kind of graft! But there are more powerful influences. Bulgaria was nearest to Constantinople, and longer subject to the Turks than any other Balkan country – the language is full of Turkish words, and the popular life of Turkish customs. Then Russia's freeing her in 1876 turned the entire trend of Bulgarian thought toward her mighty Slav brother. There was also a group of intellectuals, fighting to free Macedonia, who imbibed republican ideals in France. And lastly, Bulgarian army officers, scientists, teachers, journalists, and politicians, for the last fifteen years have studied almost exclusively in Germany.

An hour by automobile from Sofia lies a typical Bulgarian village. The fields around it are owned and farmed communally by the inhabitants, except for the lands belonging to the monastery at the top of the hill. A wild mountain stream tumbling down the ravine turns the wheels of fourteen mills, where the peasants grind their corn; and since the mills all charge the same price, and the highest mill had no trade at all, the peasants and the monks together have agreed to abolish all mills, and build a single large one run by electricity generated by the stream, to be owned in common by the village. Broad, comfortable houses with tile roofs, built of wood or stone or baked clay, straggle along the cobbled streets. Every one seems happy and prosperous, for in Bulgaria each peasant can own five inalienable acres of land, and, as in Serbia, there are no rich men. At the end of the street is a big, fine public school, with room for all the children, and teachers trained in Germany. Telegraph and telephone, train and automobile road connect it with the city. And these evidences of organization and progress are to be seen all over Bulgaria. King Ferdinand and the group of scientific experts with which he has surrounded himself are chiefly responsible for all this. The Bulgars are loyal, honest and easily disciplined, in contrast to the anarchistic Serbs. Centuries of Turkish tyranny have helped to prepare them for the hand of the organizer.

I know three derisive stories told by the peasants of other Balkan peoples about Bulgars for seven hundred years, which illustrate the Bulgarian character better than anything I could say.

A Bulgar who had been mowing late in his fields went home at night with his scythe over his shoulder. Coming to a well, he looked down and saw the moon reflected in it. 'Good God!' he cried, 'the moon has fallen into the well. I must save it!' So he put his scythe into the water and pulled. But the scythe caught in the rocks of the well. He pulled and pulled and pulled. Suddenly the rock gave way and he fell on his back. Above him in the sky was the moon. 'Ha,' said he with satisfaction, 'I have rescued the moon!'

Four Bulgars walking across the fields came to a pond with a willow-tree bending over it. Wind rustled the leaves and the peasants stopped to look at it. 'The tree's talking,' said one. 'What is it saying?' The others scratched their heads. 'It probably says that it wants a drink,' replied another. Filled with pity for the poor thirsty tree, the Bulgars climbed out on the branch and weighed it down into the water. It broke and they all drowned.

The Bulgarian army, so goes the story, had been besieging Constantinople for two years without the slightest result. They took counsel together and decided to push down the wall. So the soldiers strung themselves all around the city with their back to the wall and began to push. They pushed and sweated with all their strength – they pushed so hard that their feet began to sink into the ground. Feeling something give way, the whole army shouted: 'Just a little more now! Keep on pushing! She's moving!'

The Bulgarians were originally a Mongolian race, who invaded the Balkan Peninsula in the seventh century and mingled with the Slavs they found there. Under the legendary Tsar Simeon they erected by conquest an ephemeral 'empire,' which extended from Adrianople to the mouths of the Danube, northwest so as to include Transylvania and all of Hungary, then south to the Adriatic, taking in Bosnia, Herzegovina, Montenegro, Serbia, Albania, Epirus, and Thessaly – and east to Thrace. Two hundred years later, a Serbian 'empire' under the mythical Tsar Dushan had conquered the same territory and subjugated the Bulgars. In the thirteenth century the Bulgars predominated again, and in the fourteenth the Serbs had their turn. Twice during this time Bulgarians laid siege to Byzantium. I mention this to explain Bulgarian 'national aspirations' on 'historical grounds' – like all Balkan 'aspirations,' they are practically boundless.

But the Bulgars are really very simple people, without guile. Why, then, did they enter the war on the side of Germany and Austria? And to go further back, why did they break the Balkan Alliance and provoke the second Balkan War? It is again a question of 'aspirations.'

The Macedonian question has been the cause of every great European war for the last fifty years, and until that is settled there will be no more peace either in the Balkans or out of them. Macedonia is the most frightful mix-up of races ever imagined. Turks, Albanians, Serbs, Rumanians, Greeks, and Bulgarians live there side by side without mingling – and have so lived since the days of St Paul. In a space of five square miles you will find six villages of six different nationalities, each with its own customs, language, and traditions. But the vast majority of the population of

Macedonia are Bulgars; up to the time of the first Balkan War no intelligent Greek or Serbian or Rumanian ever denied this. Almost all of Bulgaria's great men have come from Macedonia. They were the first people, when Macedonia was a Turkish province, to found national schools there, and when the Bulgarian Church revolted from the Greek Patriarch at Constantinople – no other Balkan Church is free – the Turks allowed them to establish bishoprics, because it was so evident that Macedonia was Bulgarian. Ambitious Serbian nationalists followed the Bulgarian example of establishing schools in Macedonia, and sent *comitadjis* there to fight the Bulgarian influence; but Serbian scientists and political leaders recognized for a century that Macedonia was peopled with Bulgarians. The Serbians did not spread south; they came from the north and spread east through Bosnia, Herzegovina, Dalmatia, and beyond Trieste – and that way their logical ambitions lie.

During the last years of Balkan turmoil under the Ottomans, when the Great Powers were bawling for reform in the European *vilayets*, and the end of the Turkish Empire was in sight, Greece also sent *comitadjis* to Macedonia to wage an underground bandit warfare on the Serbs and Bulgars, with the hope of eventually getting a slice. But up to the outbreak of the Balkan War no responsible Greek ever dared to claim Macedonia on any other but 'historical' grounds. Constantinople, parts of Thrace, Asia Minor, and the European littoral of the Ægean and Black Seas were claimed by Greece because Greeks lived there. But that was all.

Even in the treaties of the Balkan Alliance that preceded the war of 1912, Serbia recognized Macedonia as Bulgarian. Mr Milanovitch, the Serbian premier who helped draw the treaties, said: 'There are districts which cannot be disputed between us. Adrianople ought to go to Bulgaria. Old Serbia north of the Char Planina Mountains ought to go to Serbia. Most of Macedonia will be Bulgarian. But a strip of eastern

Macedonia ought to be given to Serbia. And the best thing will be to leave the division to the Emperor of Russia as arbitrator.' And this was inserted in the treaty. Greece also accepted the principle of Bulgarian dominance.

When the Balkan conflict exploded, Bulgaria, with her superior army, was to leave a strong force in Macedonia, and aid Serbia with more troops if she found things difficult. But, on the contrary, it was Serbia who sent aid to the Bulgars in Thrace; this, Serbia called 'the first violation of the agreement.' Adrianople fallen, the Bulgars pressed on, amazed at their success. They said they would stop at a line drawn through Midia on the Black Sea to Enos on the Ægean; but the Turks tried so frantically to make peace that they broke the armistice, and drove straight for Constantinople. Only Tchataldja stopped them, and they might finally have stormed that if events in their rear hadn't taken a disquieting turn.

In the meanwhile the Serbians and Greeks, who had occupied all of Macedonia, Epirus, and Thessaly, were jealous of the boundless Bulgar ambition. Nothing in the Balkan Alliance had given Bulgaria the right to seize the capital of the Eastern world. Together Greece and Serbia had conquered the western *vilayets*, and they didn't see why they should give up territory fairly won to any powerful Balkan Empire – no matter what the treaties were. So they made a secret treaty and quietly went to work to Grecianize and Serbianize their new territories. A thousand Greek and Serbian publicists began to fill the world with their shouting about the essentially Greek or Serbian character of the populations of their different spheres. The Serbs gave the unhappy Macedonians twenty-four hours to renounce their nationality and proclaim themselves Serbs, and the Greeks did the same. Refusal meant murder or expulsion. Greek and Serbian colonists were poured into the occupied country and given the property of fleeing Macedonians. Bulgarian school-teachers were shot without mercy, and Bulgarian priests given the choice of death or conversion to the Orthodox religion. The Greek newspapers began to talk about a Macedonia peopled entirely with Greeks – and they explained the fact that no one spoke Greek, by calling the people 'Bulgarophone' Greeks or 'Vlaquophone' Greeks. The Serbs more diplomatically called them 'Macedonian Slavs.' The Greek army entered villages where no one spoke their language. 'What do you mean by speaking Bulgarian?' cried the officers. 'This is Greece and you must speak Greek.' Refusal to do so meant death or flight.

Bulgaria concluded a hasty peace with the Turks and turned her attention westward. The Serbs and Greeks were evasive – they declared the Balkan Alliance had been broken by their ally. Bulgaria called upon the Tsar to arbitrate, but Serbia, in possession of far more than she ever had dreamed of gaining, realized that she had powerful friends: Russia, alarmed at the gigantic ambition of her protégé, and Austria, who wanted no powerful state in the Balkans. Finally Tsar Nicholas agreed to settle the question; but just as the two delegates were about to start for St Petersburg, Bulgaria took a step that justified the fears of the Great Powers, alienated the world's sympathy, and lost her Macedonia. Without warning, her armies suddenly attacked the Serbs and the Greeks and marched on Salonika. The Bulgarian people was not consulted. The news came as shock to the cabinet, whose policy was one of conciliation and peace. Consternation and fury broke loose in Sofia. Who had given the order? There was only one person who could have done so, and that was King Ferdinand.

King Ferdinand is a regular romantic Balkan King. He perpetually sees himself riding into Constantinople on a white horse – the Tsar of an immense, belligerent empire. And as I write this he has again hurled his people against their will into a war from which they cannot emerge except as losers.

I saw it all. I was in Sofia when the Entente Powers made their offer, and from then off and on until the end. The Allies offered as the price of intervention all of Serbian Macedonia to the Char Planina Mountains, Thrace, and diplomatic support for the recovery of Grecian Macedonia and Silistria. The Central Powers would give Macedonia, part of Serbia, Silistria, free access to Cavalla and Salonika, and a slice of Turkey to be ceded immediately. Germany told Bulgaria that she need only effect a junction with the German forces through Serbian Macedonia, and then she could turn all her attention to occupying these territories; while the Allies wanted her to attack the Turks, and wait for compensation until after the war. The Bulgars clamoured for immediate occupation. . . . The Allies replied that they would guarantee her countries for her by occupying the line of the Vardar with Allied troops. But the Bulgarian Government was sceptical of promises to be redeemed 'after the war.'

The premier, Mr Radoslavov, said on July 15: 'Bulgaria is prepared and ready to enter the war immediately absolute guarantees can be given her that . . . she will attain . . . the realization of her national ideals. The bulk of these aspirations are comprised in Serbian Macedonia, with its Bulgarian population of one and a half millions. It was pledged and assigned to us at the end of the first Balkan War, and it is still ours by right of nationality. When the Powers of the Triple Entente can assure us this territory, and assure us that our minor claims in Grecian Macedonia and elsewhere will be realized, they will find us ready to march with them. But these guarantees must be real and absolute. No mere paper ones can be accepted. Only certainty on this point can induce our people again to pour out their blood.'

In that he had the country with him, for there is a very decided public opinion among the Bulgarian peasants. In the first place more than half a million Bulgarians fled from persecution in Macedonia under Turks, Greeks, and Serbs and were scattered throughout the villages of Bulgaria, forever preaching the liberation of their country. In the middle of the summer half the population of Sofia was composed of Macedonian refugees, and you could visit a camp in the outskirts of the city where sixteen thousand of them lived under tents, at great expense and annoyance to the government. While I was in Sofia in September, there arrived five thousand Bulgarians who had been taken prisoners by the Austrians after being forced to serve in the Serbian army – returned with the compliments of the Emperor Franz Joseph. Every day the press was full of bitter tales brought by the refugees, and expressions of hatred against the Serbians; the Serbian press responded as bitterly, accusing the Bulgarians of raiding across the frontier, burning and slaughtering. Both were true. To offset this hatred there was the traditional love and gratefulness – very strong among the peasants – to Russia the Liberator, and the memory of the generation who had seen her armies rout the Turks.

Bulgarian statesmen are just as they are in Rumania; they play the game of personal ambition and personal profits – with the important difference that in Bulgaria they must wheedle the people, and are subject to an unscrupulous and irresponsible monarch who has real royal power. All Bulgarians were agreed on the programme of regaining Macedonia; they only differed on the question of which group of Powers could give it to them. As Mr Joseph Herbst said to me: 'If Zululand would give us Macedonia we would march with Zululand!' A bitter and exhausting struggle went on between the two parties – between hatred of the Serbs and love for Russia. The Radoslavov government showed itself benevolent toward the Central Powers in a hundred ways – for instance, by allowing the military censorship to suppress six pro-Ally newspapers on the ground that they were 'bought with Russian gold.'

By an agreement of all political parties at the outbreak of the European war, power to act was left in the hands of the government, and the *Sobranié* adjourned indefinitely. But as the government's attitude became defined, the growing opposition demanded the calling of Parliament to consider the country's position. This the King absolutely refused to do, for he knew that the majority of the country was still pro-Ally. In its desperation the Liberal government was forced to a trick. The provinces of New Bulgaria were electing their first deputies, and they were so gerry-mandered that all the twenty deputies were Liberals. How the voters felt about it was made plain when a confidential man journeyed south to find out what side the peasants would like to fight on. 'You give us guns first,' they replied threateningly, 'and we'll show you which side we'll fight on!' In spite of the twenty, however, there was still a majority against the Germans when Bulgaria went to war.

As I passed through Sofia in the middle of August the pro-Ally sympathizers were jubilant. Mr Guenadiev, leader of the Stamboulovist party, seemed to think Bulgaria would accept the last offer of the Entente Powers, to which Serbia had conditionally agreed. Mr Guechov, chief of the Nationalists, talked of a coming demonstration in force by the opposition, to compel the summoning of the *Sobranié*. And Mr Malinov of the Democratic party believed that his country knew how fatal to Bulgarian predominance would be the German drive eastward.

But when I returned two weeks later all was changed. The Duke of Mecklenburg had twice visited the King, the Turco-Bulgarian secret treaty had been signed, the first gold instalment of an immense German loan had arrived, and Mr Guechov told me that the Central Powers were now urging Bulgaria to attack Rumania, in case attempted negotiations between Austria and Serbia came off. 'If the Germans come through Serbia to our frontier,' said Mr Guenadiev, 'what can our small army do against them? We do not want to be another Belgium.' A politician who had once told me with glowing approval how the peasants loved Russia, now seemed lukewarm. 'The peasants are very simple folk,' said he; 'they remember Russia the Liberator, but they are not intelligent enough to realize that freeing Bulgaria was merely a step in the Russian march toward Constantinople. You and I know better; we understand that the peasants will do what they are told, and that a people needs thoughtful leaders.' And he hurried away with an important, furtive air.

In the first week in September the *Opoltchenié*, or Macedonian Legion, composed of refugees, was called to the colours 'for forty-five days' training.' No one was fooled. The government press breathed double hate against the Serbs, and cried: 'Macedonians! The hour is at hand to free your country from the oppressor!' Sixteen thousand Macedonians were summoned – sixty thousand responded, and with them some fifteen thousand Albanians, and ten thousand Armenians who had been given asylum from Turkish persecution. A grand demonstration was arranged with true Bulgarian thoroughness; the new volunteers, all slow, exalted faces, and rough, brown homespun, surged through the streets cheering and singing behind their war-worn flag. They knew that they were to head a Bulgarian invasion of Macedonia. In twenty speeches delivered from the balcony of the Military Club, from the steps of the *Sobranié*, and from the Tsar Liberator monument, they were told so.

Next Sunday, September 6, was the national holiday, celebrating the thirtieth anniversary of the union of the Bulgarian kingdom. The printed programme of the parade announced that the *Opoltchenié* and the troops of the garrison of Sofia would participate; but on Saturday night a Bulgarian wood merchant told me that he had received an order from the government to unload twelve railroad cars full of timber in four hours, and turn them over to the government. Late in the evening most of the cab horses in the city were seized by government quartermasters. That very night the Macedonians mysteriously disappeared; and when the parade began in the morning the garrison of Sofia – horse, foot, and artillery – had also vanished, except for two companies. In the afternoon there was a grand patriotic demonstration by civilians, punctuated with bellicose speeches; in the evening a torchlight procession of students singing Macedonian songs. My, how full of politicians and journalists was the Grand Café de Bulgaria that night! But, in spite of the national holiday and the critical situation of events, there was no excitement whatever. There never is in Sofia – the Bulgars are an unemotional people. Even the demonstrations were methodical, organized, and directed like flocks of sheep. The party chiefs and politicians refused to be interviewed – and when that occurs in Bulgaria, things are serious indeed. Too late the Opposition leaders were scurrying around for support to stop the resistless march of events.

The last act of the *coup d'état* was brief and dramatic. On Friday, September 18, the Opposition leaders, representing six out of the eleven Bulgarian parties, had a conference with the King. Tsanov, representing the two Radical parties, Danev the Progressive Liberals, Stamboliisky the Agrarians, Guechov the Nationalists, and Malinov the Democrats, were received by his majesty in the presence of his secretary, Doctor Dobrovitch, and the Crown Prince Boris. Malinov, in his speech, said that the military situation in Europe and the political situation in the country made it extremely dangerous for Bulgaria to enter the war on either side at present. He believed firmly in continued neutrality; but if the government thought that entrance in the war would help realize the national ideals, his constituents desired that it should be on the side of the Entente Powers. Stamboliisky then presented a memorandum signed by himself and his colleagues, which respectfully demanded:

First. That the government should take no action without calling the *Sobranié* and consulting the wishes of the country.

Second. That before any action was taken a coalition

cabinet should be formed (after the model of the English and French war governments), with an enlarged number of ministers to represent the eleven political parties.

Third. That the Crown should present to the government in power the demands of the Opposition, with the indorsement of the Crown.

Guechov took the floor, pointing out by means of figures and calculations the inevitable final victory of the Entente Powers. 'The moment for our entrance into the war is unripe,' he said. Tsanov followed with a speech along the same general lines; and after a discussion precising the details of the memorandum, the King, Prince Boris, and Doctor Dobrovitch withdrew for a private discussion.

When they returned it became apparent from what Doctor Dobrovitch said that the government had made up its mind to a course of action, on the basis of information which could not be made public.

'What most concerns the people of this country,' burst out Stamboliisky, 'must remain a secret then?'

'I had no idea that you represented the people of this country, Mr Stamboliisky,' said the King. 'Why is it that you have never come to see me before?'

'Because the democratic principles of my party forbid it,' said Stamboliisky; 'but I waive principles when the country is in danger. And let me remind your Majesty that dynasties which thwart the popular will do not last long!'

'My head is old,' replied the King, 'and not of much value. But you had better take care of your own!'

In vain Malinov and Guechov tried to quiet things. By this time Tsanov had lost his temper and joined Stamboliisky, and 'for a while,' said an imaginative observer, 'they all kicked each other's shins.'

Finally the King rose and said very sternly: 'Gentlemen, I shall present your demands to the government. I can tell you that we have decided on a policy which will be thoroughly carried out at any cost. Mr Stamboliisky, I am happy at last to have made your acquaintance!'

Two days later we left Sofia for Nish, and three days after that the Bulgarian mobilization was announced.

Twenty

SERBIA REVISITED, AND GREECE

Fifteen minutes out from Sofia the train plunges again into mounting defiles between ever more towering hills, through tunnel after tunnel. Stony peaks coloured wonderfully in reds and browns and subtle greys seem animals crouching, so living is their texture. Southward the crinkled Balkans march across the sky, blue with distance. It is a breeding-place of hard men and fighters. Two hours, and we are over the divide, screaming down beside a stream that leaps in cascades. A dry, hot, little valley opens out, ringed around with arid mountains; there lies Tsaribrod, the last Bulgarian station, piled high with heaps of army supplies and buzzing with troops. A neat little town with substantial houses and public buildings, two factories, good roads running east and north, schools, electric lights, and a sewer system. A neat little station paved with concrete, where the ticket-agent who was so cordial when we stopped there four months ago, leans from his window to shake hands. The train roars through a tunnel, and twists between precipitous hills. Where they open out a little, arid and quivering with heat, lies Pirot, the first town in Serbia.

What a contrast even between these two first cousins – Bulgars and Serbs! The town straggled out, an overgrown village, all deep, wide houses roofed with Turkish tiles; no school visible. On the dirt platform before the ramshackle wooden station, a customs officer, the station-master in gold-lace uniform with a sword, a policeman in blue with red facings, and a sword, too, and two army officers, were having an animated discussion, entirely oblivious of the train. The rapid, flexible eloquence of the Serbian language struck on our ears like a jet of fresh water. Around them in easy familiarity crowded peasant soldiers in shabby grey uniforms, sandals, and the distinctive crushed-in cap of the Serbian army, listening and joining in the argument.

'Mr Pachitch!' cried the station-master vehemently: 'Mr Pachitch is no true Serbian! His father was a Bulgarian and his mother was a Turk! Who couldn't make a better prime minister than any Young Radical?' He pounded himself on the chest. 'Why I myself –'

The customs officer slapped the major on the shoulder, and burst into a shout of laughter. All the soldiers laughed, too. Down at the end of the station fence, reservists of the last call were coming through a gate, one by one, while a sergeant, called their names on the roster and ticked them off. Old men and young boys they were, in every variety of improvised uniform, tattered sandals on their feet – but all with the military cap and all equipped with new rifles. A boy who could not have been more than sixteen, so drunk that he could hardly stagger, reeled through with his peasant mother holding him upright. The tears streamed down her face; she wiped his sweating face with a handkerchief and straightened his lapels, and patted him twice on the chest. Growling, he made for the sleeping-car. A policeman grabbed him by the arm. 'Forward!' he yelled; 'get forward into the box car!' Without a word the boy threw his arms around the policeman and they fell to the ground, a waving mass of arms and legs. Everybody laughed. An incredibly aged man with one arm came hobbling up on a stick and touched a grey-haired giant who bore a rifle. He turned and they kissed each other on the mouth. Tears ran down the old man's face. 'Do not let the Bulgars through!' he shrilled....

The customs officer came into our apartment. He simply glanced at our passports and never touched the baggage.

'You came from Sofia?' he said eagerly, sitting down and offering cigarettes. 'What is the news? We've been hearing exciting rumours here. Is Bulgaria going to war? She'd better not – we'll march to Sofia in two days!'

'But if Austria and Germany attack you?'

'Pooh, they tried it once! Let them all come! Serbia can whip the world! . . .'

Ahead of us, as the train rattled along, rose a great chorus from five box cars full of soldiers. They were singing a new ballad about the Bulgarians, which began:

'King Ferdinand, the Bulgar, got up one day in his palace in Sofia and looked out the window,
And he said to his son, the Crown Prince Boris: 'My son and heir, it is a fine day and the Serbian army is very busy,
So I think if we attack their women and children we may not be defeated. . . .'

One's first impression on crossing the Greek frontier is of a mob of money-changers, boot-blacks, venders of chocolates and fruit and last week's papers – shrewd, brown little traders of harsh, quick speech and keen eyes. Three years ago there were no Greeks whatever in this arid mountain valley of southern Macedonia; now it is all Greek. That is what happens in every new Greek country; all but the lowest peasants tilling the soil are forced out by the most bitter economic competition – and even they are working for Greeks. The Rumanians are gay and graceful; the Bulgars honest and friendly; the Serbs witty, brave, and charming; after these the Greeks seem a stunted, unfriendly people without any flavour.

I think I must have asked a hundred Greek soldiers what they thought of the war. Now the salient characteristic of Balkan peoples is bitter hatred of the nearest aliens. The Greeks hated the Serbians normally, but when they spoke of the Bulgars it was in terms of torture and burning alive.

Venezelos they idolized almost to a man; but I found that they would even vote against him, for they thought he meant to force them into war – and the Greeks did not want to fight. But Greeks are very sentimental; you only have to wave a flag and shout 'glory' to them, and they will go to war for a good cause or a bad one. Greek ambitions are limitless. They consider themselves the heirs of Periclean Athens, of the Byzantine Empire, the conquests of Alexander the Great, and the far-flung colonies of the ancient Greek city-states. An editorial paragraph from a Greek newspaper displays their ordinary frame of mind:

'Greece, which has a history five thousand years old, and is the mother of Western civilization, should not let itself be surpassed by nations who have managed to assemble their children under their hegemony, as Piedmont dominated Italy, as Prussia dominated Germany. The Hellenic nation should not show itself incompetent, powerless, and inferior to certain new states, such as Austria-Hungary, Bulgaria, and Turkey, which are so many mosaics constituted in Europe by barbarians coming from Central Asia.'

And this in face of the fact that the new Greek provinces are inefficiently and corruptly governed, and that Athens itself is a hotbed of lies and bribery. A typical·example is the Greek railroad official who was bribed by Germans to hinder the mobilization of the Greek army. And remember, that the first time the *casus federis* of the Greco-Serbian treaty was ever invoked Greece refused to fulfil her obligations...

The last day I was at Salonika a great cloud of black smoke appeared at the foot of the gulf; a little destroyer steamed full speed for the city and anchored off the *quai*. Three boats were landed, containing English officers in campaign uniform, with the red tabs that mark Staff officials, twenty-five boxes and trunks, and a couple of British marines carrying rifles with fixed bayonets. The baggage was piled in the street and the officers went into the Hotel de Rome. In fifteen minutes the rumour was all over the town that Sir Ian Hamilton was in

Salonika. Wild excitement seized the Greek officials. Around the two sentries guarding the baggage prowled a solemn, uneasy circle of policemen. A dense mass of townspeople stood silently watching. Hot wires clamoured the news to Athens. Frightened officials cried: 'What does it mean? What shall we do?'

In the meantime we had run into the King of England's Messenger on his way home through Italy with despatches from the Balkans. He was pretty reasonably mellow with much Scotch and soda, as we went to lunch in the Hotel de Rome.

Five tables away from us sat the general himself – a tall, bronzed, solid Englishman with a grey moustache – and all his Staff. He and the King's Messenger bowed to one another. A few minutes afterward a waiter came to our table.

'General Hamilton would like to speak with the King's Messenger.' Our friend rose, reeling slightly, and went over. Pretty soon he came back, holding on to chairs and piloting himself with difficulty. He sat down at the table and grinned.

'It is too, too funny,' he said weakly. 'The old duffer wants me to go immediately to Athens and ask the British ambassador for instructions.

'Damme,' he said to me, 'what the devil have they sent us here for? Here I am – and not a word of instructions. What the devil do they want me to do?'

That night we took ship for Piræus and home. Next morning, steaming down between far islands that lay like clouds on the sea, we met twelve transports full of British troops on their way to Salonika.

INDEX